the NAKED VEGAN

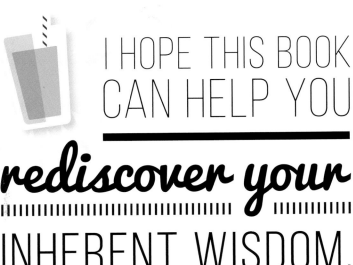

I HOPE THIS BOOK CAN HELP YOU

rediscover your

INHERENT WISDOM,

INFINITE POTENTIAL

and best possible HEALTH

the NAKED VEGAN

140+ TASTY RAW VEGAN RECIPES FOR HEALTH AND WELLNESS

MAZ VALCORZA

MURDOCH BOOKS

SYDNEY · LONDON

CONTENTS

how a
PHARMACEUTICAL SALES MANAGER
FOUNDED A
VEGAN RAW-FOOD
cafe

There once was a nurse-turned-pharmaceutical sales manager in Sydney who had always eaten whatever she wanted, partied hard, chain smoked, exercised enough to 'stay fit' and didn't think very much about the repercussions of her actions.

One day, she decided to take up yoga, because it seemed like a great way to get a bit more coordination and a toned butt. Little did she know that this snap decision, made out of curiosity and vanity, would change her life forever.

The pharmaceutical sales manager loved yoga so much, she studied to become a yoga teacher. One yogic philosophy that really resonated with her was that of *ahimsa*, which translates as 'non-violence' or 'non-harm'. This principle seems pretty straightforward: don't walk around hurting others. She soon came to realise that non-violence included avoiding injury to *all* living beings, both directly and indirectly — and that changing what she consumed as food was one of the most significant ways to ensure she was doing as little harm as possible on a daily basis.

So she decided to adopt a plant-based diet — specifically a vegan one, which differs from a vegetarian diet by avoiding not only animal flesh of any kind, but also all animal-derived products, such as eggs, dairy and honey.

She knew a plant-based diet could definitely provide all the essential nutrients, so she started researching nutrient-dense vegan options. Then she came across the concept of 'raw' food and it piqued her curiosity. What on earth was 'raw' pizza — was the dough just not baked? Can you eat more than just a bunch of carrot sticks and dip? Luckily the answer was no, and yes, respectively.

She began experimenting with online recipes, and came to find 'raw' food so delicious, quick and easy that she started sharing recipes through her own online blog.

When she came up with the idea of making vegan treats such as her Mango float cheezecake (see page 170) to sell to small cafes in her spare time, the owner of her yoga studio let her use their kitchen space... one thing led to another... and soon enough she was given a life-changing opportunity to leave the pharmaceutical world and open Sydney's very first organic, raw, vegan cafe.

That girl was me, and I'm so grateful to everyone who has helped me on this journey and supported what Sadhana Kitchen is all about: making delicious, mindful, healthy food more accessible, and encouraging our customers along their own journey with every bite.

These days, Sadhana Kitchen hosts a series of unique experiences, including a signature 'raw vegan high tea', a seven-course raw food degustation, raw cleanses, raw catering and lunch delivery services.

Sādhanā (pronounced sah-da-nah) is a Sanskrit term that translates as 'one's conscious spiritual practice'. Your *sadhana* is your daily ritual: something you do consistently and consciously to enliven your every day. At Sadhana Kitchen, we hope to share how eating ethical, healthy and delicious food can help us connect with our personal wisdom. By eating kindly and consciously every day, we remember to be more mindful in all our daily choices, to pay more attention, and to celebrate the things we enjoy and feel good about. By using delicious and beautiful raw vegan food as this reminder — as our *sadhana* — we nudge our lives in a happier, more purposeful direction.

FACEBOOK.COM/SADHANAKITCHEN ◆ TWITTER.COM/SADHANAKITCHEN
INSTAGRAM @SADHANAKITCHEN ◆ WWW.SADHANAKITCHEN.COM ◆ WWW.MAZVALCORZA.COM

I WAS A CHILD WHO ATE
SPAM FROM A CAN

People often ask me how I became interested in raw food, how I found myself living this lifestyle, and whether it's difficult to maintain. For an honest answer, I need to revisit my childhood and explain what eating was like for me growing up.

When I was very young, I was incredibly fussy. Dad had to come up with strategies to get me to eat what was on my plate. He would divide the plate into sections and I had to eat at least half; I'd sit there for ages, struggling to get it down. Of course, I would spread everything out across the plate as thinly as possible, so I would have to eat far less than was intended.

Fast forward to my early teens, when I developed the voracious appetite I have now. I still remember the day I became a 'food monster'. I was in a large food court and Mum gave me $20 to get something to eat. Usually I'd get a medium serve of chips, and that would be enough — but this day was different. I just couldn't find enough food to satisfy my hunger. I ordered two entire meals from a chicken joint, and a double cheeseburger meal from a fast-food outlet. I ate all of it, and that became the norm for me for the next decade.

My parents are Filipino, and for us a standard meal consisted of Spam (yes, the one from the can!), eggs and garlic rice. Filipinos eat quite a meat-heavy diet, with lots of white rice to balance the strong flavours. We also like to celebrate our many special occasions with *lechón* (a pig on a spit). Food is a huge part of our culture, and the easiest, quickest and most delicious way we show each other love.

Growing up, I honestly didn't know many vegetables besides potatoes. I loved potatoes, especially with corned beef (also from a tin!) and onions. It wasn't until I left home that I began to notice all the different vegies that were actually available. It sounds extreme, but by no means were my parents doing a bad job — they just fed us the same food that they'd been fed when they were growing up.

So, you can imagine their horror when I told them I had taken up yoga, and that not only did I no longer eat meat, I had become *vegan*, meaning I didn't eat any animal products at all. Filipino restaurants tend to be challenged by the concept of 'vegetarian' food — when I ordered a vegie dish at a Filipino restaurant in New York, it arrived at the table with minced pork in it anyway. I remember looking at the waiter and saying, 'I'm sorry, but I asked for no meat,' and he, with utmost sincerity, leaned in and whispered, 'Yes, maam, but how else will you get the flavour?'

Working as a nurse and then in pharmaceutical sales, I had been exposed to the big business of healthcare. Even then I was taken aback by the pharmaceutical industry's power and influence, and how much profit there is to be made, particularly from the ongoing pharmaceutical treatment of lifestyle diseases. I am very aware of how such companies have helped produce a plethora of medical advancements, but I couldn't help feeling there were also loads of drugs being marketed to treat problems that might be improved by simply eating well and exercising.

My new way of eating and my daily yoga practice had my mother questioning whether I had become a Hare Krishna. Many worries emerged: how was I to be catered for at family gatherings? What was I meant to eat when we went out? Who was ever going to marry a vegan? The standard concerns.

After making every vegan recipe I could get my hands on, even I began to wonder if there was more variety and excitement to the vegan diet. I'd been buying vegan versions of all of the junk food I used to eat, and ordering one mock meat dish after the other... and it was less than satisfying. Then along came 'raw' food, and I was hooked. Raw food was vibrant, beautiful and fresh. I began eating a wider variety of food, and more fruits and vegetables than I had ever eaten in my life. And everything was so delicious, I didn't feel I was missing out on anything, and it made me feel so good. I had loads more energy, my skin became

ALL WE CAN DO IS EDUCATE OURSELVES, TRY OUT A BUNCH OF THINGS AND SEE WHAT WORKS BEST

brighter, my mind clearer, and the food was quick and easy to prepare. This was a huge bonus, because my career back then involved lots of travel and left me with little spare time.

I also experienced my fair share of trials — not knowing what to eat when I went out with my friends, having my family think I'd gone crazy, even people who were downright rude about my new lifestyle choice and attacked me for it. People have always been afraid of what's different — but why fear positive change?

However, the way to most people's hearts is through their stomachs, and with a little pre-planning, and a whole lot of making awesome dishes for everyone to try, I managed to spend time with family and friends and not be a total pariah. My boyfriend at the time also became vegan and helped me open Sadhana Kitchen.

So, in time, my parents went from freaking out to meeting me halfway, and helped support my new lifestyle with considerate little gestures. One memorable attempt was at a large family gathering, where they cut the head off the pig on a spit, and from a whole fish, and replaced the heads with faces made of creatively sliced vegetables, so it wouldn't upset me so much. The fish's new head was made of julienned carrots with raisin eyes and a sliced celery mouth. The pig was given a whole iceberg lettuce head, cherry-tomato eyes, carrot ears and a maniacal sultana smile. Not particularly comforting, but I had to hand it to my mother for trying.

These days, my parents and brother drink green smoothies every day, have cut out most meat from their diets, and occasionally eat seafood. It's amazing what happens when people see and feel 'healthy'. It's powerful when people start to take sovereignty over their own wellbeing and make more conscious choices for themselves, the beings we share this planet with, and Mother Earth herself.

So, how do I feel when I see Spam these days? While I'd never touch it again, it is associated with many happy childhood memories and shared family bonding sessions. To me, it signifies how far I have come. It tells me that we all have different backgrounds and experiences that colour our current viewpoint. It reminds me that there is no 'one size fits all approach', and that all we can do is educate ourselves, try out a bunch of things and see what works best for us.

WHY BE HEALTHY?

Seriously, do I really need to be healthy? What actually is the point of it all?

When I first started getting into my yoga practice and changing my diet and lifestyle, I'd be asked this question all the time. And it really made me think: what actually is the point?

For me, being as healthy as I could be meant I'd be as happy as I could be — and I mean, who doesn't want to be happy? I was a really sickly child. I had pretty bad asthma, I had chest infections any time the weather changed, I'd always catch whatever was going around, and was generally quite frail. I was taking asthma maintenance medication right up until I became vegan. Not long after making the change, however, I no longer had a tight chest, persistent cough or any wheezing. I no longer got sick during the change of seasons and, amazingly, I'd be fine when people around me were knocked sideways by colds and flu.

It has now been about five years since I've needed to take any pharmaceutical medication. If I do ever feel sick these days, my symptoms are much less severe and my recovery time is super quick. I really feel I have been able to prevent illness and heal illness with the food I eat.

Life can be challenging and busy enough — so, being sick when you can otherwise avoid it just doesn't make sense to me. And when you're feeling your best, there is very little standing in the way of living the life you want.

LET FOOD BE THY MEDICINE, AND MEDICINE BE THY FOOD. HIPPOCRATES

How often do we hear others, and maybe even ourselves, complain about feeling run down, or not having enough energy? When you live a healthy lifestyle, your body and mind get taken care of, so you can go about your day with more freedom and vitality.

Our bodies are the vehicles we use every day to navigate life. It's a simple concept, but easy to forget. How our body feels every day is a major contributor to how we experience our lives, and to the overall quality of our life.

How was your day at work? How was your weekend? Whatever you did and whoever you were with, I'll bet it probably sucked if you were feeling tired, hungover, bloated, irritable, distracted, or just generally gross. Many things can contribute to such uncomfortable and all-too-common feelings ruining our days, but it's pretty clear to me that the food we eat is a major player. Get that right and you should notice the difference: more days feeling happy, friendly and more content, whatever you are doing.

THE TYRANNY OF CHOICE

We live in a world where we are spoilt for choice. It is widely accepted that having the ability to make choices in life is important and beneficial. Some might think that if having the ability to choose is positive, then the more choices the better. However, recent evidence suggests that having the ability to choose benefits us, but only to a point. Several assessments of wellbeing by social scientists suggest increased choices and affluence can actually result in decreased wellbeing.

American psychologist Barry Schwartz, in his book *The Paradox of Choice*, distinguishes between 'maximisers', who always aim to make the best choice possible, and 'satisficers', who aim for choices that are good enough, regardless of the options available. Perhaps surprisingly, he found having too many choices can have negative effects, including regret about declined opportunities, regret about options that have been chosen, and high expectations, which make it easy for experiences to fall short of what we had imagined. Compared with satisficers, maximisers often experienced less satisfaction with life, were less optimistic and more depressed.

What does all this have to do with living a healthy lifestyle, eating well and being well? Simply that there are so many eating plans, diets, programs, supplements, lifestyles, exercises and health experts out there that one can be forgiven for feeling overwhelmed and not knowing where to start. It is also easy to understand why some people become obsessive about their lifestyles, to the point that the entire practice is no longer healthy or positive.

At Sadhana Kitchen, people often ask us: What is the absolute best type of food to eat? What is the best diet to follow? What is the best exercise to do? Is paleo better than vegan? Should I eat carbs? Should I quit sugar? Do I need to be 100% raw? Should I only eat bananas?

The endless number of choices can leave people feeling defeated before they've even begun — or completely fanatical for fear of missing out on that elusive 'very best' choice. Neither of these outcomes results in a happy life. I have found that this is one of the reasons people find making healthier lifestyle changes so difficult — they become paralysed and confused by the number of choices, many of which seem contradictory and confounding.

This is why it's so important to work on the wisdom within, while also staying open to the fact that with greater knowledge and experience, you may change your tune from time to time. It's okay to just try being vegan, or eating raw, for a little while. Maybe you'll come back to it later, maybe you won't. Either way, you're learning more about what works best for you, empowering you to make better choices for yourself.

THE KISS PRINCIPLE

Most systems work best if they are kept simple, instead of being made complicated. It's just like the KISS principle: Keep It Simple, Stupid.

The same applies to creating a healthy lifestyle. A good place to start is to look at what you *really* want, then compare this to what you *think* you should want. For example, 'I want... to be the fittest and healthiest version of myself' rather than, 'I think I should... lose some weight and hit the gym five times a week.' These are two very different goals. It's easy to think we need that photoshopped model's body, when all we really want is just to look a little happier, and feel a little more confident and energised.

Be honest about where you are right now, compared to where you want to be, then set a goal to achieve what you want. Your goal could be as simple as: 'I want to be happy eating well, and do activities I enjoy that also keep me fit.'

Then identify your first steps that you can stick to. Don't choose too many things to change all at once; just pick maybe one or two things that seem interesting or fun. Maybe it's a class you've heard of, or trying a vegan dish that looks particularly tasty. These simple steps can go a long way towards creating a happier lifestyle. Better than creating a complicated five-year plan — unless, of course, that is precisely what works for you!

WE ARE WHAT WE REPEATEDLY DO. EXCELLENCE, THEN, IS NOT AN ACT, BUT A HABIT. ARISTOTLE

Bad habits can sometimes be hard to break — but good habits can also be easy to form, if you set yourself up for success. When something makes you happy, then it's pretty easy to stick with, so the trick is to create positive habits that also bring you joy.

When people share with me their struggles to become and then stay healthy, a big obstacle is the inability to form lasting positive habits. Often this is because they set their sights too high to begin with, or their new healthy habit is unrealistic to achieve.

When it comes to the crunch, the outcome has to be worth the effort. Kicking bad habits is a challenge, so you need to accept from the outset that it won't necessarily be easy, but it will be worth it.

SETTING YOURSELF UP FOR SUCCESS

Here are a few simple tools for forming and sticking with positive habits that I've learnt along the way.

Break it down. Your overall goal is important, but if you are feeling a bit overwhelmed or not sure where to even start, it can be helpful to break the whole thing down into small, mini goals that are easily achievable. So, if your overall goal is to be healthy, you can break that down into eating well, exercising and looking after your mind.

So, depending on where you're at, your mini goals may be:
⋇ I will prepare and eat one healthy meal this week.
⋇ I will go for a 30-minute walk in the park after dinner twice this week.
⋇ I will listen to a guided meditation before going to sleep once this week.

You'll get a feeling of satisfaction from achieving your mini goals, and at the same time get a taste of the benefits your new habits can offer you.

Plan for the times when you just want to give up. Let's face it — new habits are especially fragile, and so many things can unfold in our days that can affect our motivation levels and self-belief. So always have a back-up plan for those shitty days. It may be as simple as sharing your goals with a friend, asking them to help keep you accountable by scheduling motivational phone calls or texts.

Another effective strategy is to figure out exactly what is causing you to abandon ship. For example, you're meant to go home and eat a healthy dinner you've prepared the night before, but you have to attend a work function instead. Missing that goal of eating well at home could trigger a chain of events where you lose motivation and get further away from your goal. I mean, you know there's going to be free booze at this function and hot chips at the bar, so might as well give up now, right?

Not necessarily. Instead of fretting, feeling bad and giving up, you can say: 'When I get to the work function, I will choose the most nutritious thing on the menu and enjoy it.' We aren't always going to be in complete control, and part of being happy is learning to roll with the punches by adjusting our frame of mind and making the most out of each moment.

Which brings us back to some helpful advice from American psychologist Barry Schwartz. Rather than always searching for that elusive 'best' choice, just find one choice that meets your core needs — then stop thinking about it. Learn to accept 'good enough', and don't worry about what you might be missing: FOMO (fear of missing out) can be paralysing and is not conducive to mental clarity and peace, both of which are essential for a healthy and happy life. Teach yourself to focus instead on what is being satisfied by the selection you make.

Another helpful strategy is to control your expectations. The adage, 'Don't expect too much, and you won't be disappointed' may sound clichéd, but is useful advice if you want to be more satisfied with life. We can all cultivate practices that will help us find peace in our current situation. For example, yoga is a tool that I use to help me stay mindful and present. I have found that dissatisfaction and distress can only occur if I'm in dismay about the past, or worried about the future. So by trying to be present, I find myself not being too attached to specific outcomes and more able to make the most of each moment instead.

CONNECTING WITH YOUR INNER WISDOM

What is personal wisdom? It's our intuition, our instincts, our innate ability to seek true health and happiness and make conscious choices. We all have it in us and we all inherently know what's good for us.

When it comes to food, the way our bodies and minds react can let us know whether or not what we have consumed has been good for us. Have you ever felt immediately weighed down, tired and sleepy after a meal? Ever woken up after a huge night drinking and felt like death? Ever eaten that whole block of chocolate, ran around like a crazy person for an hour and then crashed for the rest of the day? I know I have.

Our bodies are remarkable machines that have an intelligence that allows us to be truly happy and healthy, if we just take the time to pay attention. Just as we have adverse reactions to what isn't so great for us, our bodies have built-in mechanisms to seek out what is good for us. After eliminating what we are addicted to from our diets, such as processed foods and refined sugars, we naturally start to crave foods that are actually good for us. All it takes is to honestly pay attention to your body and allow it to guide you to the healthiest and happiest version of yourself that you can be.

TAKING SOVEREIGNTY OVER YOUR HEALTH & WELLBEING

You might be thinking, dude, what does that even mean? In short, it's about taking back power, responsibility, authority and influence over your health and happiness.

Taking it back from whom? Basically everyone who has a lot to gain from the way you choose to live your life.

Perpetuating your health problems is big business, and the upsetting truth of profit-driven business (as opposed to values-driven business) is that the more unhealthy and unhappy you are, the easier it is to sell you things you don't need — even though the most effective and sustainable solution to such lifestyle diseases is to create a healthy lifestyle that you enjoy.

Some of the biggest killers in our modern world are 'lifestyle' diseases, which only come about because of the lifestyle choices we make. Diseases such as obesity and type 2 diabetes can be prevented by eating the right foods and exercising regularly. A lot of the items we refer to as 'food' in our society are unrecognisable from what real food is actually supposed to be. A great deal of profit is made from selling cheap, processed, high-sugar items that provide little to no nutritional or health value. Many of the bodies we see posted on billboards and social media feeds are not realistic for us to achieve, or sustainable for long-term health; this makes it easy to unknowingly set unrealistic goals and expectations, and then be disappointed even when we do succeed at creating a healthy and sustainable lifestyle for ourselves.

That's why it's so important to cultivate your own personal wisdom. Only you know what you really need to be healthy and happy, and only you can discern what choices provide the best results. Every single person is unique; there is no 'one size fits all' approach.

Instead of becoming overwhelmed by all the different information you come across, use it as an opportunity to connect with your inherent wisdom. Try things out for yourself. Think, feel and see what resonates with you most. Free yourself from the fears and insecurities around you and be inspired to take responsibility for how your actions affect you and the world in which you live.

OH BABY, I LIKE IT RAW: WHAT IS RAW FOOD?

Raw food is like magic. It grows in the ground and, through the wonder of nature, becomes this vibrant, nutrient-dense stuff we can eat — vegetables and fruits, and plant-based wholefoods. This is real food, grown the way nature intended, and filled with all the nutrients that the human body needs — not just to survive, but to thrive.

Raw foods are free from animal products and haven't been heated over 40–46°C (104–115°F). This is important as most enzymes — as well as many essential vitamins and minerals — become diminished or destroyed when heated at temperatures higher than this. Enzymes are made of various proteins and are essential to all bodily functions, including digestion. Our bodies produce some enzymes, but we also get enzymes from the food we eat.

If you eat food with its enzymes still intact — as they are in raw foods — your body doesn't have to use its natural enzyme reserves to digest the food, which keeps them free to fulfil all the functions they were meant for: repairing and regenerating your body.

Nature has thankfully accounted for our need of digestive enzymes by placing them within each unique food — so if you're eating broccoli, there are exactly the type of enzymes within its chemistry that allow you to digest it. In the same process, you are absorbing the

maximum amount of other vital nutrients, such as proteins, vitamins and minerals. This is why eating raw foods is so beneficial.

Personally, I've found that incorporating a large amount of raw, organic foods into my diet has resulted in many positive changes, including increased energy levels, clearer skin, more muscle tone and improved mood. Enhanced concentration, productive sleep, better digestion, weight loss and reduced risk of heart disease are some of the other health benefits you may enjoy.

Without a doubt, including an abundance of organic, plant-based wholefoods into your lifestyle — whether you are paleo, or raw, or a panda! — is going to do you a whole lot of good.

WHY BOTHER WITH ORGANIC?
THE REAL COST OF FOOD

One of the biggest misconceptions about eating organic food is that it's too expensive — so what are our eating choices really costing us?

When we talk about the cost of food, we shouldn't just consider what we pay at the check-out. Most produce these days is grown using chemical pesticides and fertilisers, in order to yield greater volumes at cheaper prices. However, commercial farming practices contribute to soil degradation, meaning subsequent crops need to be further chemically treated to yield any produce, and many studies have also suggested that such produce has a lower nutritional content than an organically farmed equivalent.

Too often with mass-produced conventional food, we hear about farmers being treated unfairly, our soil eroding and our waterways becoming polluted. If that wasn't enough, that conventional produce is often processed until it's completely distorted and mixed with various chemical additives and filler ingredients devoid of nutrition. What we see at the end of the process is often a pretty package that's cheap and convenient to buy. But the reality is that most people are not paying fair or real prices for their fruit, vegies and grains — and in the end, consumers are paying with their health and wellbeing.

What people often don't realise is that the nutrients in food come from the soil that it is grown in. Food from degraded soil may still look good, but will contain fewer nutrients every year. Sad times. Part of attaining ultimate health is making ultimate choices to consume ultimate food. Our health and wellbeing are worthy investments. When we choose organic, pesticide-free produce — which is often tastier and denser in nutrients, and kinder to the

farmers as well as our bodies — we are investing in our long-term vitality and choosing not to contribute to the ongoing destruction of the environment.

For me, all of that is worth the small difference in price between conventional and organic produce. At Sadhana Kitchen, all of our ingredients come from organic producers where possible.

As the old adage goes, we are what we eat. Literally.

IT DOESN'T HAVE TO COST THE EARTH

Purchasing organic, plant-based wholefoods can be affordable in the short term, and save you a whole lot of time and money by keeping you healthy and happy over the long term.

You can grow some of your own organic produce on your balcony or in your backyard. Herbs are a great place to start and are fairly low maintenance.

These days, organic farmers markets and groceries are popping up all over the place. Most of these have a direct relationship with the organic farms they source from, or are the farmers themselves. By supporting them, you'll also get really good prices for the freshest food. And you'll be eating with the seasons, rather than buying produce that has been cold-stored for lengthy periods. Seasonal produce will be the cheapest, most delicious and most nutritious produce you can get at any time.

Why not start a food swap in your area, or join a community garden, and buy or trade locally whenever you can? Many people have an occasional excess of backyard produce and would be happy to see their lemons go to good use, rather than fall off the tree and rot.

Another great idea is to join an organic food cooperative — many of them offer volunteer positions and give great discounts in return. Or you could buy food in bulk and distribute it among friends. It's often much cheaper to buy larger quantities of items such as nuts, seeds and superfoods — and you'll also help reduce waste by using less packaging. You can join the social media pages and mailing list of your favourite companies for great deals and giveaways.

Sometimes you'll be able to find second-grade produce; so long as it is fresh, it is just as delicious and nutritious as first-grade produce, but often much cheaper simply because it doesn't look quite as pretty.

And don't forget to use your freezer space. When fruit and vegies are fresh and cheap, you can chop them up and freeze in snap-lock bags, ready to be turned into smoothies each day. While heat degrades and destroys enzymes, freezing doesn't affect the nutritional content.

PERSONAL WISDOM...
WE ALL HAVE IT IN
US AND WE ALL
INHERENTLY KNOW
WHAT'S GOOD FOR US

When organic produce isn't available, you can cleanse conventionally grown fruit and vegetables of pesticide traces by soaking them in a mixture of filtered water and apple cider vinegar — 1 tablespoon apple cider vinegar per 1 litre (35 fl oz/4 cups) water — for 20–30 minutes.

EATING FOR WELLNESS & BEAUTY

There is mounting evidence that the standard Western diet is not the best for longevity and wellness; billions of dollars are being spent each year on pharmaceutical drugs to treat diseases, including obesity, diabetes, heart disease, stroke and cancer, that could perhaps more easily have been avoided through addressing our diet and exercise.

Government dietary guidelines throughout the West, and from the World Health Organization, are consistently urging us to consume more vegetables, fruits and legumes and less saturated fat, sugar and salt.

While it's important to do your own research, it's not always feasible to keep abreast of all the latest evidence, especially when a lot of it seems contradictory and quick-changing. If reading scientific papers is your thing, then great, please do more of that and let your deductions and understanding help you to create your own culture of health. When seeking health advice, always ask yourself, how healthy is the person giving you advice?

The key lies in realising that ultimately it is up to you to use your own faculties — your brain, your personal wisdom, your intuition and your personal experience — to create the best outcomes for yourself.

There are some things in life that we just inherently know. In the same way we instinctively understand that it's probably not a good idea to walk off the edge of a 20-storey building, we also know it's a safe bet that eating fresh fruits and vegetables is going to be much better for us than chowing down into highly processed foods filled with chemical additives.

Whatever your current lifestyle, eating more organic, plant-based wholefoods — especially fresh fruits and vegetables — will most likely benefit you.

POWERING AWAY ON RAW FOODS

Raw foods can sound daunting when exploring them for the first time — but the good news is that anyone can start incorporating more raw foods into their diet by simply eating more fruits and vegetables.

And rest assured that there are more than enough nutrients in raw foods to keep our bodies in optimum health. Plant sources of **protein** can easily provide all the essential amino acids we need; for example quinoa, almonds, flax, hemp and chia seeds are all rich sources of protein that the body can more easily digest than meat. As long as we eat enough variety of raw foods throughout the course of a day, our bodies can synthesise essential amino acids into complete proteins, making protein deficiency highly unlikely. Similarly, plant sources of **iron,** such as broccoli and bok choy (pak choy), also contain high levels of vitamin C, which the body requires to absorb iron properly; other good sources of iron include pumpkin seeds, sesame seeds, quinoa, cashews, almonds, spirulina and dried apricots. As for **calcium,** kale, collard greens, almonds, sesame seeds, chia seeds, watercress, hazelnuts and dried nori all contain over 150 mg of calcium per 100 g (3½ oz) serve, compared with 118 mg in cow's milk. And **vitamin B12,** which is mainly found in animal-derived foods and can be lacking in some vegetarian diets, can be obtained in small amounts from nutritional yeast, sea vegetables, fermented foods and some mushrooms; just to be sure, I take a daily plant-based organic vitamin B12 supplement from my local health food store.

Your own journey to raw — or to better eating in general — will be unique, but a good place to start is simply ensuring that each day you have at least one meal abundant in leafy greens and at least one whole piece of fruit. When you're ready, try out the strategies below.

- ❖ Eat dark, leafy greens as often as you can. Nutrient-dense, but low in calories and rich in fibre, these are one of the few items you can consume in unlimited quantities — and something most people don't eat enough of. Wake up with a green smoothie every day, then have some salad with (or for) lunch, and a side salad with your dinner.
- ❖ Enjoy cold-pressed vegie juices or smoothies throughout the day. This will flood your system with nutrients, fill you up and make you less likely to reach for that greasy burger or packet of chips.
- ❖ Snack on fruit and vegies instead of processed foods. Make your own trail mix using your favourite nuts and seeds, shredded coconut and dried berries. Snack on a punnet of strawberries or blueberries, or a banana or pear. Kale chips, vegie sticks and dip, nori rolls filled with avocado and sprouts... there are so many yummy

things you can enjoy when you're feeling peckish that are both filling and serve a nutritional purpose.

⚬ Try out kick-ass healthy dressings and dips. If your diet is filled with processed foods, or you don't eat much fresh produce, it may take time for your tastebuds to readjust and appreciate the amazing flavours of nature. So in the meantime, eating vegies with delicious yet nutritious accompaniments will make the process more enjoyable. You'll find heaps of easy recipes in this book!

⚬ Eat the rainbow. Every day, eat as many varieties of fruits and vegetables as you can, in as many vibrant colours as you can; this will help ensure you are getting the widest spectrum of nutrients into your system. If you're eating out and there aren't any filling salad options, choose meals that are loaded with vegies, such as vegetable stir-fries.

As you become more familiar with raw foods, you can begin creating so many amazing dishes and treats. You'll find over 140 tasty and easy recipes in this book. Give them a go — I promise your body will thank you for it!

THE GIFT OF MINDFULNESS

Since starting my yoga practice, my attitude towards how I consume food has completely changed.

In my previous job, I was lucky to grab something on the go in between appointments, catching taxis, catching planes and trying to get the most out of every work hour. This inevitably meant that every time I was feeding myself, I wasn't paying much attention. Did I chew my food properly? Did I enjoy what I was eating? How did it make me feel? I wasn't ever really sure, because I was trying to refuel as quickly as possible in between more 'important' things in my day.

My yoga practice opened my mind to the idea of being 'present' within every moment. Because food is such an intrinsic aspect of our lives, it makes so much sense that we should especially choose to be present when sitting down to a meal. This has so many benefits, from creating a more positive relationship with food, to becoming more mindful about how you are fuelling your body, to giving yourself adequate time to digest food properly and receiving the maximum benefits.

When I reflect on how my day went, it's often the delicious and beautiful meals that I enjoyed the most. All the more reason, then, to slow down and pay attention while it's happening.

When you are about to eat or drink, try the following:

⚬ Sit down if you can; if not, make sure you're as comfortable as you can be.

⚬ Take a moment to smile and be grateful for the opportunity and the privilege to nourish yourself, when so many others are lacking.

⚬ Look at the food's colours and textures — nature is pretty magical, and the fact that this stuff just grows in the ground is mind blowing!

⚬ Savour your first bite or sip. Let the flavours hit your tongue, then the rest of your senses. You're giving your body the fuel it needs in the most mindful way possible and that is pretty special.

⚬ When you're done, connect with whatever you are eating or drinking and see how it makes you feel.

This really doesn't take long and you will quickly find yourself reaping the benefits of mindful eating. In our busy society, getting back to basics, practising gratitude and acting mindfully can really go a long way in cultivating the healthiest and happiest lifestyle possible.

The beauty of incorporating more raw foods into your lifestyle is that they are incredibly good for you, simple to prepare, kind to the environment and absolutely delicious. It encourages you to be creative, expands your knowledge of the best foods on the planet and allows you to heal yourself with vibrant, mouth-watering nourishment. The healthy glow and boundless energy are just bonuses.

I really believe that what we put into our bodies every day is part of our *sadhana*. I hope this book can help you to cultivate your own *sadhana*, and through that practice, rediscover your inherent wisdom, infinite potential and best possible health.

No one has all the answers and your path will never look exactly like mine or anyone else's. Your own journey will be unique, with its own trials and tribulations. Your needs are different to mine and require an equally unique approach. The point is to learn as much as you can, while enjoying the ride. If you like what you're doing, then it's never going to be a chore or a hassle.

The good news is that living a healthy and happy lifestyle can be fun, rewarding, simple and delicious, all at the same time.

And it is totally within your reach.

GLOSSARY OF INGREDIENTS

◦ **ACTIVATED NUTS**
Raw nuts that have been soaked in salted water to break down their enzyme inhibitors, making them easier to digest. Here is a quick soaking guide for the nuts and seeds in this book: *almonds* 8–12 hours; *Brazil nuts* 3 hours; *buckwheat groats* 6 hours; *cashews* 2–3 hours; *hazelnuts* 7–12 hours; *linseeds (flax)* 6 hours; *macadamias* 7–12 hours; *sunflower seeds* 7 hours; *walnuts* 4 hours.
After soaking, thoroughly rinse your nuts or seeds, then use straightaway, or dehydrate at 40°C (105°F) until completely dry, seal in snap-lock bags and store in the fridge or freezer to stay fresh.

◦ **APPLE CIDER VINEGAR**
Choose 'raw' apple cider vinegar that still has the 'mother' culture in it. These are the cobweb-like strands of proteins, enzymes and good bacteria that give the vinegar a cloudy appearance.

◦ **ARAME** A type of seaweed from the kelp family, commonly used in Japanese cuisine. Seaweed is a super-nutritious plant food, packed with micronutrients such as calcium, iron, zinc, manganese, vitamins A and K, and iodine.

◦ **BLACK SALT** Also called *kala namak*, *kala noon* or *sulemani namak*, this grey-coloured volcanic salt naturally contains sulphur, giving it a pungent 'eggy' smell and flavour.

◦ **CACAO POWDER**
see raw cacao powder

◦ **CAROB POWDER**
A potent antioxidant food, carob powder is ground from the dried, sweet edible pulp of the pods from the carob tree. It is rich in fibre, vitamin E, potassium and magnesium.

◦ **CAT'S CLAW**
A powerful antiviral and anti-inflammatory herb from Peru.

◦ **CHIA SEEDS** These tiny seeds are a powerhouse of essential nutrients. They contain 20% complete protein (including all nine essential amino acids), five times more calcium than dairy milk, three times more iron than spinach, seven times more vitamin C than oranges, and significant levels of omega-3 oils, potassium, antioxidants and fibre.

◦ **CELTIC SEA SALT** *see* Himalayan pink salt

◦ **COCOA POWDER**
see raw cacao powder

◦ **COCONUT NECTAR**
Low in fructose, and made from the sweet sap of the coconut blossom, this raw low-GI nectar is rich in minerals and contains 17 amino acids (protein building blocks).

◦ **COCONUT SUGAR** Also made from the sweet sap of the coconut blossom; the liquid is crystallised by being evaporated at low temperatures, keeping it a raw product.

◦ **DULSE FLAKES** Dulse is a seaweed rich in vitamins A, B1, B2, B3, B6, B12, C and E, and minerals including potassium, calcium, magnesium, phosphorus, chromium, iodine and zinc. Adding dulse flakes to dishes gives them a 'fishy' taste.

◦ **FILTERED ALKALINE WATER** As water makes up 55–75% of our bodies, it's important we drink the best water possible. Natural spring water is best. Tap water is naturally acidic, but you can buy filters that alkalinise your water.

◦ **FRENCH GREEN CLAY POWDER** A powerful internal detox supplement, used widely as a cosmetic product. For the recipes in this book, make sure you use food-grade French green clay, easily sourced online. Green clays remove toxins from the body, build immunity, and contain a range of minerals and phytonutrients.

◦ **GOJI BERRIES** These dried red berries are rich in nutrients, containing the highest protein level of any fruit, 15 times as much iron as spinach, and more protective carotenoids than any other food.

◦ **GREEN SUPERFOOD POWDER** Use any blend of superfood powder that contains high-quality greens such as spirulina, chlorella, alfalfa, wheatgrass and barley.

◦ **HEMP SEEDS** Sold in health food stores, hemp seeds are a complete plant protein, the only known plant source of the 'sunshine vitamin' (D3), the richest source of plant omega 3 and 6 fatty acids, and high in other nutrients such as iron, calcium and zinc. Although not considered psycho-active in any form, and legal to eat in nearly every country in the world, please check the laws in your country before using, and omit from recipes if necessary.

◦ **HIMALAYAN PINK SALT OR CELTIC SEA SALT**
Regular salt, often called table salt, is highly refined and contains additives such as anti-caking agents. Himalayan pink salt and Celtic sea salt are free of impurities and contain traces of potassium, iron, magnesium and calcium.

◦ **HORSETAIL** An anti-inflammatory, antiviral, antimicrobial and antioxidant herb that builds and supports immunity.

◦ **KELP NOODLES** Clear noodles made from the seaweed, kelp. They are nutrient dense, gluten free and raw. Soak them in filtered alkaline water for 30 minutes to soften, then rinse and drain thoroughly.

❀ **LUCUMA** A Peruvian fruit with a creamy citrus flavour, lucuma is a rich source of beta-carotene, vitamin B3 and iron. It also contains significant amounts of unrefined carbohydrates, fibre, and other vitamins and minerals. The powdered form can be used as a natural low-GI sweetener.

❀ **MACA POWDER** Part of the radish family, maca is a Peruvian root vegetable rich in vitamins, minerals, enzymes, nearly 60 phytochemicals, and all the essential amino acids. It is considered an adaptogen, meaning it supports hormonal functioning and helps the body cope with stress.

❀ **MEDJOOL DATES** These plump, fleshy dates are often called the 'king of dates'. We use them a lot in raw recipes for their natural sweetness, and as a binding ingredient due to their stickiness. Packed with fibre, vitamins and minerals, they contain 50% more potassium per gram than bananas.

❀ **MESQUITE** Usually sold as a powder, ground from the ripe seed pods of the mesquite tree. It is high in protein (16%), rich in calcium, magnesium, potassium, iron, zinc, lysine and fibre, yet low in carbohydrates and fat.

❀ **MISO** A paste made from fermented and aged soya beans. Opt for unpasteurised miso, which has probiotic benefits.

❀ **NUTRITIONAL YEAST** An inactive form of yeast, used widely by vegans for its cheesy flavour. You don't have to be vegan to enjoy its taste or nutritional benefits, which include B vitamins, folic acid, selenium, zinc and protein.

❀ **OREGANO OIL** Cold-pressed from the leaves and flowers of the herb oregano, this oil has potent immune-boosting properties and is sold in organic food stores. Just ensure it is food grade, as not all essential oil mixtures are safe to ingest.

❀ **PAU D'ARCO** An Amazonian herb with potent antifungal, antimicrobial and immune-boosting properties.

❀ **PROBIOTIC POWDER** A rich source of beneficial bacteria, probiotics help build immunity and support digestive health, aiding with the digestion and assimilation of food. Look for vegan brands.

❀ **PSYLLIUM HUSK** A soluble dietary fibre, from the *Plantago ovata* plant. Psyllium husk acts as a natural thickener and binder, soaking up water in the gut and aiding bowel movements.

❀ **RAW CACAO POWDER** This is made from cacao beans, and is not heat treated above 40°C (105°F). Cocoa powder, sold in most supermarkets, is made from the same cacao bean, but is heat treated. In its raw state, cacao is very antioxidant and nutrient rich, with the highest magnesium content of any food. It is also rich in omega-6 fatty acids, iron, chromium, zinc, copper and vitamin C, as well as mood-boosting compounds such as serotonin, tryptophan, PEA (released in the brain when we fall in love!) and anandamide (the bliss chemical). However, once you heat cacao, the nutritional content deteriorates significantly, so always use raw cacao powder when making chocolate. You'll find it in most health food stores.

❀ **SHILAJIT EXTRACT** An important adaptogenic and rejuvenative herb in Ayurvedic medicine. It is a potent antioxidant, detoxifier, antibiotic and anti-inflammatory, and supports the nervous system, mental function, strength, endurance and libido.

❀ **SOY LECITHIN** An oily substance found in soya beans. It is an emulsifier, meaning it binds liquids to fats, helping to achieve the creamy textures found in our raw cakes.

❀ **SPIRULINA** Claimed to be the most nutrient-rich whole food on the planet, with over 100 nutrients, this aquatic blue-green algae contains about 60% protein and is rich in iron and antioxidants. It is commonly sold in powdered form.

❀ **SPROUTED BROWN-RICE PROTEIN POWDER** Made from sprouted, fermented brown rice, this plant-based source of protein is easier to digest than animal protein.

❀ **STEVIA** A natural sweetener, made from the stevia plant, which is part of the sunflower family. It is 200 times sweeter than sugar and contains no calories.

❀ **TAHINI** A paste made from ground sesame seeds. A rich source of calcium, potassium, iron, phosphorus and magnesium, tahini also contains high levels of B vitamins, vitamin E and protein.

❀ **TAMARI** A gluten-free, naturally fermented Japanese soy sauce.

❀ **TRUFFLE SALT** Sea salt that has been combined with pieces of black or white truffle, an underground fungus prized for its earthy flavour. Truffle salt adds depth and body to all kinds of dishes.

❀ **VANILLA POWDER** This is made from dried, ground vanilla beans and adds wonderful flavour to desserts. We prefer this to vanilla essence or extract, as it is a wholefood and raw.

❀ **WAKAME** A dried edible brown seaweed or kelp, commonly used in Japanese, Korean and Chinese cuisine. It is extremely nutritious and low in calories.

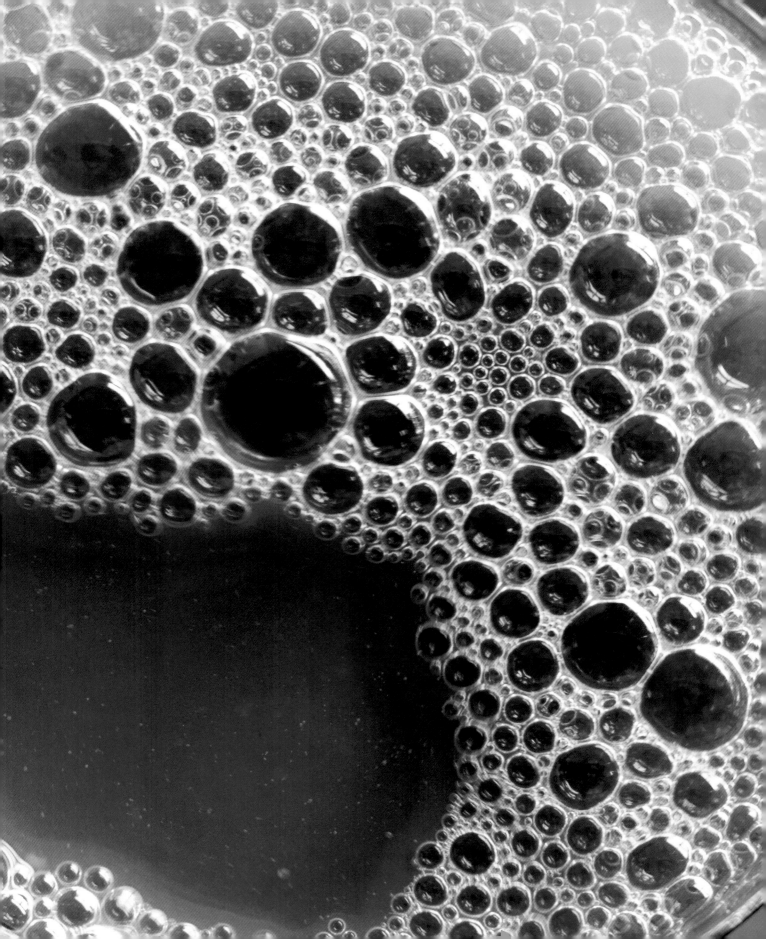

COLD-PRESSED JUICES & SHOTS

GET JUICY!

Conventional centrifugal juicers use high speed and friction to grind the juices out of fresh produce. This heats the juice, destroying some vital enzymes that aid optimum digestion of its other nutrients. By contrast, cold-pressing preserves these health-giving enzymes by using a low-speed pressing motion to squeeze the juice out of fruits and vegetables, so their nutrients are more easily assimilated by the body.

There is no need to peel thin-skinned produce such as apples, carrots, ginger and turmeric if they are organic (just wash them well first), but I would peel conventionally grown produce.

The drinks in this chapter will keep for up to 72 hours in a sealed glass jar in the fridge, but for maximum nutrition and vitality are best enjoyed straightaway. Remember to 'chew' your juices, shots and smoothies, to obtain the most nutrients from them.

SADHANA WAKE-UP CALL

SERVES 1; MAKES 500 ML
(17 FL OZ/2 CUPS)

These days, after quitting the ciggies, eating plant-based foods and being more present and mindful when I am eating, I no longer crave the things I used to.

This drink is part of my daily 'sadhana'. On waking, and before yoga practice, I drink one of these to flush out my system, rehydrate my body, kick-start my metabolism and prepare for the day.

1 whole lemon (including the peel, if the lemon is organic), quartered
2.5 cm (1 inch) knob of fresh turmeric, peeled and chopped
120 g (4¼ oz/1 cup) chopped apple
pinch of cayenne pepper
250 ml (9 fl oz/1 cup) filtered alkaline water

✿ Pass all the ingredients through a cold-press juicer, adding the water last.

GREEN GLORY

SERVES 1; MAKES 500 ML
(17 FL OZ/2 CUPS)

Green juices are a great way to get a super-concentrated dose of alkalinising vitamins, minerals and enzymes into your bloodstream each day. Drinking cold-pressed juices such as these can give your digestive system a rest while your body redirects that energy into other vital processes, such as detoxification.

Use the cucumber, celery, kale, mint and lemon as your base drink, then add the extra goodness from one of the two variations given below.

350 g (12 oz/2 cups) chopped cucumber
125 g (4½ oz/1 cup) chopped celery
70 g (2½ oz/1 cup) chopped kale
2 mint springs
½ lemon (including the peel, if the lemon is organic), halved

Green staple
45 g (1½ oz/1 cup) baby English spinach leaves, shredded
1 parsley sprig

Green remedy
160 g (5½ oz/1 cup) chopped pineapple flesh
2.5 cm (1 inch) knob of fresh ginger, peeled and chopped

✿ Pass all the ingredients through a cold-press juicer, alternating the cucumber and celery with the leafy greens — the cucumber and celery have a high water content and will help the leafy greens pass through the machine.

1 SADHANA WAKE-UP CALL

2 GREEN GLORY

MANIPURA MAGIC

SERVES 1; MAKES 500 ML
(17 FL OZ/2 CUPS)

Loaded with antioxidants and vitamin C, this golden orange juice is named after the 'manipura' chakra, because of its vibrant yellow colour. Chakras are energy junctions in the 'subtle body' (non-physical body), where the energy channels meet. There are seven main chakras. Situated behind the navel, the manipura chakra is said to be the centre of vitality, clarity, self-confidence and wisdom.

2.5 cm (1 inch) knob of fresh turmeric, peeled and chopped
50 g (1¾ oz/1 cup) chopped carrot
225 g (8 oz/1 cup) chopped, peeled orange
120 g (4¼ oz/1 cup) chopped apple

❖ Pass the ingredients through a cold-press juicer, popping the turmeric in first, then alternating between the carrot and the orange when putting them through the juicer shoot. Finish with the apple, to flush out as much of the turmeric colouring as possible, for easier cleaning.

PIÑA COLADA ZINGER

SERVES 1; MAKES 500 ML
(17 FL OZ/2 CUPS)

So refreshing, this juice reminds me of being on a secluded beach in the summer with my best friends.

40 g (1½ oz/½ cup) chopped young coconut flesh
350 g (12 oz/2 cups) chopped cucumber
125 g (4½ oz/1 cup) chopped celery
160 g (5½ oz/1 cup) chopped pineapple flesh
½ lemon (including the peel, if the lemon is organic), halved

❖ Pass the ingredients through a cold-press juicer, pushing the coconut through first for easier juicing.

BLOODY GOOD ROOT

SERVES 1; MAKES 500 ML
(17 FL OZ/2 CUPS)

Beetroot contains powerful antioxidants, is low in fat, rich in fibre, and packed with vitamins and minerals, particularly calcium, iron, folic acid, and vitamins A and C. Drinking a little fresh beetroot juice is a great way to get an extra boost of nutrition each day and help your body's natural detox processes.

300 g (10½ oz/2 cups) chopped raw red beetroot (beet)
100 g (3½ oz/2 cups) chopped carrot
120 g (4¼ oz/1 cup) chopped apple
125 g (4½ oz/1 cup) chopped celery
2.5 cm (1 inch) knob of fresh ginger, peeled and chopped
2 cm (¾ inch) knob of fresh turmeric, peeled and chopped
½ lemon (including the peel, if the lemon is organic), halved

✢ Pass the ingredients through a cold-press juicer. It helps to alternate the apple with the harder root vegetables for efficient juicing.

POST-WORKOUT SHOT

SERVES 1; MAKES 60 ML
(2 FL OZ/¼ CUP)

This is energy in a shot. Down one of these after a sweat session to boost your reserves and aid recovery.

1 teaspoon cold-pressed extra virgin coconut oil
1 teaspoon coconut sugar
2 teaspoons raw cacao powder
2 teaspoons chia seeds
1 teaspoon shilajit extract
40 ml (1½ fl oz) Vanilla almond mylk (page 174)

✢ Add all the ingredients to the shot glass, stir until well combined, then down the shot.

ALKALINISER SHOT

**SERVES 1; MAKES 60 ML
(2 FL OZ/¼ CUP)**

Often the standard Western diet is very acid-forming in the body. Downing this shot, in addition to eating lots of alkalinising plant-based foods, can help return your body to a state of equilibrium.

1 teaspoon green superfood powder; one containing
   spirulina, chlorella and wheatgrass will work nicely
90 g (3¼ oz/½ cup) mixed roughly chopped kale, spinach
   and broccoli

❖ Add the superfood powder to a shot glass. Pass the kale, spinach, and then the broccoli through a cold-press juicer. Add the juice to the shot glass, stir until well combined, then down the shot.

GLOWING SKIN SHOT

**SERVES 1; MAKES 60 ML
(2 FL OZ/¼ CUP)**

French green clay has powerful detoxification effects, while cucumber has long been used both internally and topically for its skin hydrating and nourishing properties. After taking this shot, make sure you drink lots of water throughout the day to aid the body's elimination processes.

¼ teaspoon French green clay powder; make sure it is
   food-grade
1 mint sprig
45 g (1½ oz/¼ cup) chopped cucumber

❖ Add the green clay powder to a shot glass. Pass the mint and cucumber through a cold-press juicer. Add the juice to the shot glass, stir until well combined, then down the shot.

IMMUNITY SHOT

SERVES 1; MAKES 60 ML
(2 FL OZ/¼ CUP)

When I feel like I'm coming down with a bug, or everyone around me is, I down a few of these and get plenty of rest to keep any symptoms at bay. This shot is loaded with vitamins and minerals to support your immune system when it's taking a beating. It's also anti-inflammatory — great for clearing blocked noses and soothing a sore throat.

5 cm (2 inch) knob of fresh turmeric, peeled and chopped
2.5 cm (1 inch) knob of fresh ginger, peeled and chopped
¼ lemon (including the peel, if the lemon is organic)
1 teaspoon organic oregano oil; make sure it is food-grade
pinch of cayenne pepper

❀ Pass the ingredients through a cold-press juicer, then down the shot.

ENERGY-BOOSTER SHOT

SERVES 1; MAKES 60 ML
(2 FL OZ/¼ CUP)

This baby packs an energetic punch. Containing medicinal herbs such as schisandra berry and reishi mushroom, it will pick you up, without giving you a caffeine crash or the jitters. Schisandra berry extract is made from the berries of a climbing vine native to north-east China and Russia. In the East it is used as an anti-stress herb and to improve immunity, aid detoxification, support the liver and treat menopausal symptoms. Reishi mushroom extract is derived from reishi mushrooms, which have anti-allergenic, anti-inflammatory, antiviral, antibacterial, immunity-boosting and antioxidant properties. It is used for treating arthritis and is also an effective anti-stress agent.

5 cm (2 inch) knob of fresh ginger, peeled and chopped
1 teaspoon cold-pressed extra virgin coconut oil
40 ml (1½ fl oz) green tea
½ teaspoon schisandra berry extract
½ teaspoon reishi mushroom extract

❀ Pass the ginger through a cold-press juicer. Add the remaining ingredients to a shot glass, then add the ginger juice. Stir until well combined, then down the shot.

BREAK FAST

Brekky is said to be the most important meal of the day. Usually, I tuck into a Sadhana wake-up call (page 22) first thing, then enjoy 1–2 litres of my Erryday green smoothie (page 49). But when I'm feeling like a non-liquid breakfast, or if I'm meeting a friend, I turn to one of the dishes in this chapter. Many of them are inspired by the traditional favourites that we all know and love — minus the filler ingredients and refined sugar, and made only with organic plant-based wholefoods, of course!

BANANA CREPES WITH COCONUT WHIPPED CREAM, CHOCOLATE FUDGE SAUCE & BERRIES

SERVES 4

These crepes are as mouth-watering as they look and, as far as sweet breakfasts go, deliciously guilt-free. If you want to impress someone, this should do the trick. This recipe makes more than four crepes, but you can always freeze the leftovers for later use. At which point, you'll be stoked with yourself for making it so easy to enjoy an epic breakfast.

Banana crepes
4 bananas, peeled and chopped
220 g (7¾ oz/2 cups) linseed (flaxseed) meal
2 tablespoons coconut nectar
2 teaspoons ground cinnamon
125 ml (4 fl oz/½ cup) filtered alkaline water

To serve
1 batch Coconut whipped cream (page 148)
1 banana, peeled and sliced
150 g (5½ oz/1 cup) sliced strawberries
125 g (4½ oz/1 cup) raspberries
1 batch Chocolate fudge sauce (page 147)

❖ Place all the crepe ingredients, except the water, in a high-speed blender, placing the bananas in the bottom of the jug for easy blending. Blend on high-speed until smooth, adding the water as needed to reach a smooth consistency.

❖ Spread the mixture on dehydrator trays lined with non-stick sheets. Use a butter knife to score into four equal squares. Dehydrate at 40°C (105°F) for 4 hours. Flip the crepes over and score the other side, then dehydrate for another 2 hours, or until set but still pliable. (If you don't have a dehydrator, place the mixture on baking trays lined with non-stick sheets and leave in the oven on its lowest setting, with the door slightly ajar, for 1 hour. Flip and dehydrate for a further 30 minutes, or until set but still pliable.)

❖ To serve, take four crepes and place 2 heaped tablespoons of coconut whipped cream in the middle of each, running diagonally from one corner to the other. Pop some sliced banana on top, then fold the corners over, to seal the crepes.

❖ Top with another dollop of coconut whipped cream, the berries and a drizzle of the chocolate fudge sauce.

SADHANA ORIGINAL-BLEND GRAWNOLA WITH COCONUT MYLK

SERVES 4

Of the three grawnola varieties we offer at Sadhana Kitchen, I think this one is my favourite. It's delicious served on its own, and is also darn amazing coated in raw dark chocolate. I also love sprinkling some over our chia puddings (page 36) for an extra crunch.
Try not to eat it all out of the dehydrator, though. It's that good!

Grawnola
90 g (3¼ oz/1 cup) finely desiccated coconut
55 g (2 oz/1 cup) coconut flakes
550 g (1 lb 4 oz/3 cups) activated buckwheat groats
110 g (3¾ oz/1 cup) goji berries
120 g (4¼ oz/1 cup) cacao nibs
110 g (3¾ oz/1 cup) linseed (flaxseed) meal
1 tablespoon vanilla powder

250 ml (9 fl oz/1 cup) coconut nectar
3 tablespoons filtered alkaline water

To serve
1 banana, peeled and sliced
155 g (5½ oz/1 cup) blueberries
150 g (5½ oz/1 cup) strawberries
1 batch Coconut mylk (page 174)
Coconut whipped cream (page 148)

❖ In a large mixing bowl, toss together the grawnola ingredients until well combined, adding the filtered water in small amounts as needed if the mixture is too dry.
❖ Spread onto dehydrator trays lined with non-stick sheets. Dehydrate at 40°C (105°F) for 12 hours. Remove the non-stick sheets. Flip the grawnola over and place on mesh trays, then dehydrate for another 6 hours. (If you don't have a dehydrator, place the grawnola on baking trays lined with non-stick sheets and leave in the oven on its lowest setting, with the door slightly ajar, for 3 hours, then flip and dehydrate for a further 1 hour.)
❖ Once set, break the grawnola apart into small clusters and store in a large sealed container.
❖ To serve, divide the grawnola among bowls. Top with the fruit, and serve with the coconut mylk and a little coconut whipped cream.

SADHANA SIGNATURE CHIA PUDDING

SERVES 4

Chia seeds are loaded with nutrients, including calcium, iron, protein and healthy fats. They are flavourless on their own, which actually makes them very versatile, as they take on the taste whatever you soak them in. Chia puddings are a very quick, convenient and filling breakfast option that will keep you energised all morning. You can also use this base recipe with any other mylk in this recipe book and your own toppings, so you'll never get bored.

1 litre (35 fl oz/4 cups) Vanilla almond mylk (page 174)
100 g (3½ oz/⅔ cup) chia seeds
1 batch Raspberry chia jam (page 148)
1 batch Coconut yoghurt (page 78)
seasonal fruit, to serve

❖ In a large bowl, whisk the almond mylk and chia seeds together for a few minutes, to prevent lumps forming. You will see the chia seeds begin to soak up the liquid; it's important to keep stirring until the seeds have absorbed all the liquid and the mixture has thickened.
❖ Leave to set in the fridge for 20 minutes.
❖ To serve, divide the chia pudding among four bowls. Top with a generous dollop of raspberry chia jam and coconut yoghurt. Decorate with seasonal fruit and serve.

PEANUT BUTTER & JAM ACAI BOWL

SERVES 4

One of the world's richest sources of vitamin C and antioxidants, the acai berry grows wild and abundantly in the Amazon. Acai bowls are the business — bursting with nutrition, and so refreshing, especially when it's hot outside. I've become seriously addicted to this peanut butter, jam and acai combo.

Acai bowl
2 x 200 g (7 oz) packets of frozen acai berries
400 g (14 oz/2 cups) frozen chopped bananas
4 heaped tablespoons raw cacao powder
4 large medjool dates, pitted
2 heaped tablespoons organic peanut butter (or almond or macadamia butter)
250 ml (9 fl oz/1 cup) Coconut mylk (page 174)

To serve
1 banana, sliced
120 g (4¼ oz/1 cup) Sadhana original-blend grawnola (page 34)
4 heaped tablespoons cacao nibs
4 heaped tablespoons organic peanut butter (or almond or macadamia butter)
4 heaped tablespoons Raspberry chia jam (page 148)

❖ Blend all the acai bowl ingredients in a high-speed blender on high speed until super smooth, using a tamper to push the mixture onto the blades, as it's quite thick.
❖ Divide the acai mixture among four bowls. Arrange some banana slices over each one, then sprinkle with the grawnola. Top with 1 heaped tablespoon each of the cacao nibs, peanut butter and chia jam. Serve straightaway.

PEANUT BUTTER
& JAM ACAI BOWL

BEST EVER
BREAKFAST SCRAMBLE WRAPS

SERVES 4

If you're after a pretty breakfast that tastes as good as it looks, this one is guaranteed to get your pals instagramming 'food porn' after brekky at yours. The black salt really helps to impart an eggy flavour to this raw vegan scramble.

Scramble
155 g (5½ oz/1 cup) activated
   Brazil nuts
75 g (2½ oz/½ cup) activated
   sunflower seeds
1 teaspoon ground turmeric
1 teaspoon smoked paprika
1 tablespoon dijon mustard
1 teaspoon black salt
125 ml (4 fl oz/½ cup) filtered
   alkaline water
1 tablespoon cold-pressed
   extra virgin olive oil
40 g (1½ oz/¼ cup) diced red
   capsicum (pepper)

3 tablespoons roughly chopped
   coriander (cilantro)
70 g (2½ oz/½ cup) finely
   diced celery
100 g (3½ oz/½ cup) seeded
   and diced tomatoes

To serve
4 Beet it wraps (page 62)
1 batch Tomato sauce (page 114)
45 g (1½ oz/1 cup) baby English
   spinach leaves

❖ To make the scramble, place the Brazil nuts, sunflower seeds, spices, mustard, salt, water and olive oil in a high-speed blender. Whiz until smooth, then transfer to a mixing bowl. Stir in the remaining scramble ingredients, until it resembles the real thing.
❖ To serve, place a wrap on a chopping board. Spread with 2 tablespoons of the tomato sauce. Top with a handful of baby spinach, and 4 heaped tablespoons of the scramble. Roll up, sealing the edges, and cut in half.
❖ Repeat with the remaining ingredients to make another three wraps. Serve straightaway.

BAGELS WITH CHIVE CHEEZE, CAPERS & PAPAYA GRAVLAX

SERVES 4

I love bagels — I'm just not a fan of the bloating, or the sudden urge to have a nap, that comes along with eating one. This recipe is really filling, and another impressive breakfast-date option if you want to score some extra brownie points.

Papaya gravlax

140 g (5 oz/1 cup) thinly sliced
   papaya (I use a mandoline for this)
2 tablespoons lemon juice
4 tablespoons chopped dill
2 tablespoons caper brine (from
   the capers used for serving)
1 tablespoon dulse flakes
¼ teaspoon Himalayan pink salt
   or Celtic sea salt

Chive cheeze

1 batch Aged macadamia
   cheeze (page 79)
3 tablespoons finely
   chopped chives
4 tablespoons chopped dill

To serve

8 Bagels (page 60)
3 tablespoons capers

✿ Place all the papaya gravlax ingredients in a mixing bowl. Carefully massage together, then leave to marinate for 20 minutes.

✿ In a separate bowl, place all the chive cheeze ingredients. Using a fork, mix thoroughly until well combined.

✿ To serve, cut each bagel in half. Place the bottom piece on a plate and spread with the chive cheeze. Add some papaya gravlax and a sprinkling of capers. Spread some more chive cheeze on the inside of the top bagels, pop onto the bottom pieces and serve.

CORN & ZUCCHINI FRITTERS WITH CHILLI JAM & SOUR CREAM

SERVES 4

This brunch favourite is just so satisfying. You can make up a huge batch of fritters and store them in the freezer, so that you can literally just warm them up in the dehydrator and throw this dish together in less than 10 minutes.

Corn & zucchini fritters

6 large zucchini (courgettes), spiralised (see Tip, page 72)
400 g (14 oz/2 cups) sweet corn kernels
80 g (2¾ oz/½ cup) diced red capsicum (pepper)
40 g (1½ oz/¼ cup) finely diced red onion
3 tablespoons roughly chopped coriander (cilantro)
2 teaspoons ground cumin
110 g (3¾ oz/1 cup) chia seed meal
1 teaspoon Himalayan pink salt or Celtic sea salt
½ teaspoon chilli powder
3 tablespoons nutritional yeast
125 ml (4 fl oz/½ cup) filtered alkaline water

To serve

90 g (3¼ oz/2 cups) rocket (arugula) leaves
1 batch Chilli jam (page 125)
1 batch Sour cream (page 78)

❖ Combine all the fritter ingredients with your hands, breaking up the zucchini into shorter pieces in the process.
❖ Divide the mixture into equally sized fritters, about 10 cm (4 inches) round, then place on dehydrator trays lined with non-stick sheets.
❖ Dehydrate for 6 hours at 40°C (105°F). Remove the non-stick sheets, flip the fritters over and place on a mesh dehydrator tray. Dehydrate for another 2 hours, or until they resemble fried fritters. (If you don't have a dehydrator, place the fritters on baking trays lined with non-stick sheets and leave in the oven on its lowest setting, with the door slightly ajar, for 30 minutes, or until crispy.)
❖ To serve, place a small handful of rocket on each plate. Top with the fritters, then dollop with the chilli jam and sour cream. Enjoy straightaway.

BREAKFAST TRIFLES

SERVES 4

Here's an awesomely quick and nutritious breakfast if you need to eat on the road. Just layer everything in a mason jar and you're good to go.

Chia pudding

4 tablespoons chia seeds
500 ml (17 fl oz/2 cups) Choc-cashew mylk (page 178)

For the other layers

1 batch Raspberry chia jam (page 148)
1 batch Coconut yoghurt (page 78)
120 g (4¼ oz/1 cup) Sadhana original-blend grawnola (page 34)
300 g (10½ oz/2 cups) sliced strawberries

❖ Combine the chia pudding ingredients in a bowl and mix well until all the liquid has been absorbed and the mixture thickens. Refrigerate for 20 minutes to set further.
❖ Grab four mason jars. In each, add two layers of each of the trifle components, starting with the chia pudding and finishing with the strawberries.

BREAKFAST TRIFLES

THE SADHANA KITCHEN BENEDICT

SERVES 4

I used to go to clubs every weekend and eat eggs benedict from a 24-hour cafe at 4 am. Post-clubbing cravings: I'd like to think we've all been there. This dish captures all the same flavours and enjoyment, without the nasty hangover and pointless calories — just nutrient-dense, plant-based deliciousness. Food is fuel for the amazing machine that is our body, and premium fuel doesn't have to lack flavour or pleasure! Try making this popular Sadhana Kitchen dish at home and impress all the babes.

Wilted spinach
1 tablespoon cold-pressed
    extra virgin olive oil
1 tablespoon lemon juice
180 g (6 oz/4 cups) baby
    English spinach leaves

Mushrooms
150 g (5½ oz/2 cups) sliced
    Swiss brown mushrooms
2 teaspoons tamari

1 teaspoon lemon juice
1 tablespoon cold-pressed
    extra virgin olive oil

Avocado eggs
1 large avocado, flesh roughly
    mashed
½ teaspoon black salt
1 tablespoon black sesame seeds
1 tablespoon white sesame seeds

To serve
4 pieces of Onion flat bread
    (page 59)
4 large pieces of Coconut bacon
    (page 128)
1 batch Hollandaise sauce
    (page 118)
sprouts or fresh herbs such as
    tarragon or dill, to garnish

❖ Start by wilting the spinach. In a mixing bowl, massage the olive oil and lemon juice into the spinach leaves, then set aside to marinate and 'wilt'.

❖ Combine all the mushroom ingredients in a bowl and set aside to marinate.

❖ To assemble the avocado eggs, use a melon baller or small ice cream scoop to form four balls of mashed avocado. Place the salt and sesame seeds in a small bowl. Roll the avocado balls in the mixture.

❖ To serve, place a piece of onion bread on each plate. Top with the wilted spinach, marinated mushrooms and a piece of coconut bacon. Drizzle with the hollandaise sauce, then top with an avocado egg. Garnish with sprouts or herbs and serve.

LEMON PROTEIN PANCAKE STACK

SERVES 4

These pancakes make for a killer post-workout meal. You can make
a whole bunch in advance, then freeze what you don't devour
for a quick on-the-go meal option when you're short on time.

Pancakes
400 g (14 oz/2 cups) peeled
and grated apple
90 g (3¼ oz/1 cup) finely
desiccated coconut
130 g (4½ oz/1 cup) buckwheat
flour
150 g (5½ oz/1 cup) macadamia
meal
55 g (2 oz/½ cup) linseed
(flaxseed) meal

2 heaped tablespoons vanilla
protein powder
4 tablespoons lemon zest
3 tablespoons lemon juice
3 tablespoons coconut nectar

To serve
1 batch Lemon curd (page 143)
1 batch Coconut whipped cream
(page 148)
75 g (2½ oz/½ cup) macadamia
nuts, roughly chopped
45 g (1½ oz/½ cup) finely
desiccated coconut
2 tablespoons lemon zest
1 batch Salted caramel sauce
(page 142)

❖ Place all the pancake ingredients in a food
processor fitted with an 'S' blade and mix until
well combined.

❖ Spoon the mixture onto dehydrator trays lined
with non-stick sheets. Using the back of the spoon,
spread the batter into round pancakes about 10 cm
(4 inches) wide. Repeat until all the batter is used,
to make 20 pancakes.

❖ Dehydrate at 40°C (105°F) for 6 hours. Flip the
pancakes over, remove the non-stick sheets and place
on mesh trays. Dehydrate for a further 2 hours, or until
set. (If you don't have a dehydrator, place the pancakes
on baking trays lined with non-stick sheets and leave

in the oven on its lowest setting, with the door
slightly ajar, for 40 minutes. Flip and dehydrate for
a further 30 minutes, or until set but still pliable.)

❖ To serve, place a pancake on each plate, then top
each with a little lemon curd, coconut whipped cream,
chopped macadamias and desiccated coconut. Repeat
the process until you have a stack, five pancakes high,
on each plate.

❖ Use an ice cream scoop to top each stack with
a generous dollop of coconut whipped cream and
lemon curd. Sprinkle with the remaining macadamias,
coconut and the lemon zest. Drizzle some salted
caramel sauce all over and fall in love.

CHOC-HAZELNUT WAFFLES

SERVES 4

Raw vegan waffles? Yep, it's a thing. A very tasty, indulgent and nutritionally dense thing. This is my idea of a radical Sunday-brunch self-care session.

Waffles
165 g (5¾ oz/1½ cups) linseed (flaxseed) meal (see Tip)
110 g (3¾ oz/1 cup) hazelnut meal (see Tip)
55 g (2 oz/½ cup) almond meal (see Tip)
400 g (14 oz/3 cups) buckwheat flour (see Tip)

200 g (7 oz/1 cup) peeled and grated apple
1 teaspoon vanilla powder
3 tablespoons coconut nectar

To serve
1 batch Choc-hazelnut spread (page 147)
60 g (2¼ oz/½ cup) roughly chopped hazelnuts
150 g (5½ oz/1 cup) sliced strawberries
1 batch Chocolate fudge sauce (page 147)

✣ Place all the waffle ingredients in a food processor fitted with an 'S' blade or a dough hook. Mix on high speed until well combined.

✣ Line a waffle maker on both sides with plastic wrap, and use it as a mould for shaping the dough into waffles.

✣ Transfer the waffles to dehydrator trays lined with non-stick sheets. Dehydrate at 40°C (105°F) for 8 hours. Remove the non-stick sheets, flip the waffles over and place on mesh trays. Dehydrate for a further 2 hours, or until the outside is set. (If you don't have a dehydrator, place the waffles on baking trays lined with non-stick sheets and leave in the oven on its lowest setting, with the door slightly ajar, for 2 hours. Flip and dehydrate for a further 1 hour.)

✣ To serve, place a waffle on each plate. Using an ice cream scoop, place a generous dollop of choc-hazelnut spread on top. Decorate with the hazelnuts and strawberries and drizzle some chocolate fudge sauce all over.

 TIP You can grind your own activated almonds, linseeds, hazelnuts and buckwheat groats into a meal or flour using a high-speed blender.

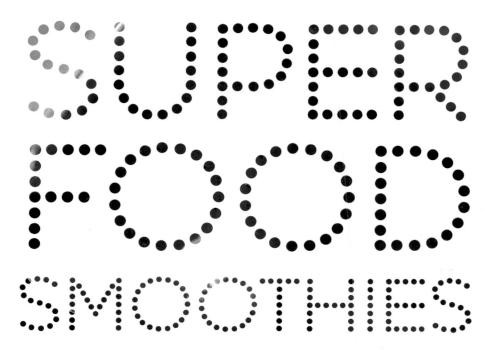

SUPER FOOD SMOOTHIES

Smoothies, unlike juices, blend fruits and vegies whole, leaving the fibre intact. When consuming fruits, fibre can be useful in regulating the absorption of fructose. Fibre also helps to keep the digestive system healthy by aiding the body's natural elimination processes. Fibre intake has also been shown to benefit diabetes, blood cholesterol levels and weight control. At Sadhana Kitchen, we use fresh organic produce and blend them up with superfoods to take their nutritional value to the next level. Think of these guys as your daily insurance policy for meeting your nutrient requirements and maximising your health.

DAILY GREEN SMOOTHIE

SERVES 1: MAKES 500 ML
(17 FL OZ/2 CUPS)

This was one of the first green smoothies I ever made, and it quickly became a staple in my household. It was also a real game-changer for my Spam-loving parents, who now drink this every single day — and if they can make the leap, heck, anyone can!

When my dad made his first green smoothie, he basically blended green vegies with water and wondered why it tasted like grass. I introduced him to freezing fruit such as bananas to add texture and flavour, which made all the difference. In time, as your body slowly starts to crave what it needs, rather than what it's addicted to, your tastebuds will learn to appreciate different flavour profiles. Until then, don't be afraid to add fruit to your smoothies.

200 g (7 oz/1 cup) chopped frozen banana
75 g (2½ oz/½ cup) chopped frozen mango
60 g (2¼ oz/½ cup) chopped apple
35 g (1¼ oz/½ cup) shredded kale
25 g (1 oz/½ cup) chopped lettuce
30 g (1 oz/¼ cup) chopped celery
300 ml (10½ fl oz) filtered alkaline water

❖ Place all the ingredients in a high-speed blender, adding the fruit first for easy blending. Blend on high speed until super smooth and drink as soon as possible.

GREEN VELVET SMOOTHIE

SERVES 1: MAKES 500 ML
(17 FL OZ/2 CUPS)

One of the cool things about green smoothies is that there are literally endless variations. This particular combination is smooth and creamy, which can make a nice change from the usual green smoothie combinations out there.

220 g (7¾ oz/1 cup) frozen strawberries
4 medjool dates, pitted
35 g (1¼ oz/½ cup) shredded kale
25 g (1 oz/½ cup) shredded spinach leaves
1 tablespoon chia seeds
1 teaspoon vanilla powder
300 ml (10½ fl oz) Vanilla almond mylk (page 174)

❖ Place all the ingredients in a high-speed blender, adding the fruit first for easy blending. Blend on high speed until super smooth and drink as soon as possible.

MAZ'S ERRYDAY GREEN SMOOTHIE

SERVES 1; MAKES 500 ML
(17 FL OZ/2 CUPS)

This green smoothie is my all-time favourite, hands down. I drink at least 1 litre (35 fl oz/4 cups) of this green goodness every day. It's delicious, filling and loaded with essential nutrients that will help you fly through your morning. The addition of green powder and probiotic powder ensures it meets your daily nutritional needs.

115 g (4 oz/½ cup) peeled and chopped orange segments
½ mango cheek, frozen, flesh chopped
35 g (1¼ oz/½ cup) roughly chopped kale
30 g (1 oz/¼ cup) chopped celery
1 heaped tablespoon Coconut yoghurt (page 78)
2 tablespoons passionfruit pulp
1 teaspoon green superfood powder
1 teaspoon probiotic powder
300 ml (10½ fl oz) filtered alkaline water

✿ Place all the ingredients in a high-speed blender, adding the fruit first for easy blending. Blend on high speed until super smooth and drink as soon as possible.

YOGINI'S GREEN SMOOTHIE

SERVES 1; MAKES 500 ML
(17 FL OZ/2 CUPS)

Especially delicious after a yoga class, this super-refreshing green smoothie is loaded with vitamin C and antioxidants, and contains healthy fats and protein. The lucuma serves as a natural sweetener and hormone regulator.

2 kiwi fruit, peeled
190 g (6¾ oz/1 cup) dried apricots
100 g (3½ oz/½ cup) chopped frozen banana
225 g (8 oz/1 cup) peeled and chopped orange segments
40 g (1½ oz/1 cup, tightly packed) chopped cos (romaine) lettuce
3 tablespoons hemp seeds
1 tablespoon lucuma powder
300 ml (10½ fl oz) filtered alkaline water

✿ Place all the ingredients in a high-speed blender, adding the fruit first for easy blending. Blend on high speed until super smooth and drink as soon as possible.

WARRIOR SMOOTHIE

SERVES 1; MAKES 500 ML
(17 FL OZ/2 CUPS)

Great as a pre- and post-workout fuel for all the warriors out there, this epic meal in a glass is packed with muscle-building, cholesterol-free protein, healthy omega-3 fats for brain function, and calcium and manganese for healthy bones.

25 g (1 oz/¼ cup) frozen blueberries
30 g (1 oz/¼ cup) frozen raspberries
100 g (3½ oz/½ cup) chopped frozen banana
1 tablespoon sprouted brown rice protein powder
1 teaspoon chia seeds
1 teaspoon cold-pressed extra virgin coconut oil
1 teaspoon mesquite powder
400 ml (14 fl oz) filtered alkaline water

❖ Place all the ingredients in a high-speed blender, adding the fruit first for easy blending. Blend on high speed until super smooth and drink as soon as possible.

MANGO MACA MADNESS SMOOTHIE

SERVES 1; MAKES 500 ML
(17 FL OZ/2 CUPS)

Mangoes are my absolute favourite fruit. I once ate a whole box of mangoes for lunch at the beach, and then had mangoes again for dinner, and I am still not sick of them! The malty flavour of maca goes surprisingly well with mango and coconut.

liquid and flesh from 1 whole young coconut
150 g (5½ oz/1 cup) chopped frozen mango
1 tablespoon maca powder

❖ Place the coconut and mango in a high-speed blender, then sprinkle with the maca powder. Blend on high speed until super smooth and drink as soon as possible.

PITAYA TROPICAL SMOOTHIE

SERVES 1; MAKES 500 ML
(17 FL OZ/2 CUPS)

Just 100 g (3½ oz) of dried pitaya (dragon fruit) contains around half your daily fibre, calcium and vitamin C requirements. Pitaya helps lower cholesterol, and also contains vitamin B3, which is great for your skin. In some countries, people who have diabetes are urged to eat pitaya to help regulate their blood sugar levels.

200 g (7 oz/½ cup) chopped pitaya
50 g (1¾ oz/¼ cup) chopped frozen banana
30 g (1 oz/¼ cup) chopped apple
55 g (2 oz/¼ cup) peeled and chopped orange segments
small handful of ice cubes
300 ml (10½ fl oz) filtered alkaline water

❖ Place all the ingredients in a high-speed blender, adding the fruit first for easy blending. Blend on high speed until super smooth and drink as soon as possible.

PINK PASSION FRAPPÉ

SERVES 1; MAKES 500 ML
(17 FL OZ/2 CUPS)

This frappé is a winner with the kids, because it's naturally sweetened with delicious fruit. It's great as a healthy frozen treat on a hot day and gives your body a nice vitamin and hydration boost.

115 g (4 oz/½ cup) peeled, chopped and frozen orange segments
50 g (1¾ oz/¼ cup) chopped frozen banana
55 g (2 oz/¼ cup) frozen strawberries
2 tablespoons passionfruit pulp
350 ml (12 fl oz) filtered alkaline water

❖ Place all the ingredients in a high-speed blender. Use the tamper to push the ingredients onto the blade, then blend on high speed until a thick frappé forms. Drink as soon as possible.

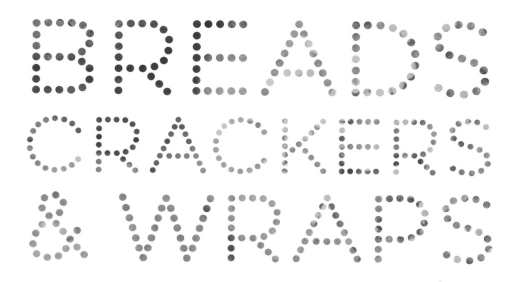

BREADS CRACKERS & WRAPS

Raw breads, crackers and wraps get a whole lot more
interesting than just the humble linseed (flaxseed) cracker.
Ideally, you would have a dehydrator to 'unbake' the
following recipes in, but if you don't have one, no sweat —
just use your oven on its lowest setting, with the door
slightly ajar, and follow the instructions as described.
I love to make big batches of these recipes and store them
in the freezer, so I can whip up meals without having to wait
12 hours for some components to be ready. A little bit of
forethought goes a long way.

SESAME & NORI CRACKERS

SERVES 4

Seaweed is one of my favourite things to snack on. It contains significant levels of iodine, a nutrient missing in many other foods. Consuming enough iodine helps healthy functioning of the thyroid gland, which is responsible for producing and regulating the body's hormones. Seaweed also contains high levels of antioxidants, calcium, and a wide array of vitamins, including A and C.

175 g (6 oz/1 cup) peeled and chopped zucchini (courgette)
75 g (2½ oz/½ cup) sunflower seeds
75 g (2½ oz/½ cup) pepitas (pumpkin seeds)
110 g (3¾ oz/1 cup) linseed (flaxseed) meal
1 teaspoon Himalayan pink salt or Celtic sea salt
1 teaspoon dulse flakes

2 tablespoons coconut nectar
2 tablespoons filtered alkaline water
2 teaspoons cold-pressed sesame oil
4 tablespoons lemon juice
2 tablespoons tamari
20 g (¾ oz/2 cups) shredded nori sheets
3 tablespoons black sesame seeds

❖ Combine all the ingredients in a food processor, except half the nori and all the sesame seeds. Process on high speed until a sticky dough forms.

❖ Turn off the food processor and stir in the remaining nori and the sesame seeds. Mix by hand until well combined.

❖ Spread the dough on dehydrator trays lined with non-stick sheets. Use a sharp knife to score the dough into the shape and size of cracker that you prefer. Dehydrate at 40°C (105°F) for 8 hours, flipping them over and removing the non-stick sheets after 4 hours, or when the exposed side is firm. (If you don't have a dehydrator, place the dough on baking trays lined with non-stick sheets and leave in the oven on its lowest setting, with the door slightly ajar, for 2 hours, then flip and dehydrate for a further 1 hour.)

❖ Cut the crackers to shape by cutting along the scored lines. The crackers will keep in an airtight container for up to 7 days, or in the freezer for several months.

PIZZA BASES

MAKES 8 PIZZA BASES

I love pizza. Seriously, almost as much as the Ninja Turtles love pizza. Raw pizzas are one of the many dishes that are actually as good, if not better, than the regular version. This pizza base is a solid foundation for the best raw pizzas in all the land.

400 g (14 oz/4 cups) almond meal
40 g (1½ oz/½ cup) psyllium husks
220 g (7¾ oz/2 cups) linseed (flaxseed) meal
4 teaspoons Himalayan pink salt
2 teaspoons dried oregano
2 teaspoons dried thyme
2 teaspoons dried basil
125 g (4½ oz/1 cup) cauliflower florets
85 g (3 oz/½ cup) peeled and chopped zucchini (courgette)
250 ml (9 fl oz/1 cup) filtered alkaline water

❖ Combine the almond meal, psyllium, linseed meal, salt and dried herbs in a large mixing bowl.

❖ Blend the cauliflower, zucchini and water together in a high-speed blender until smooth. Pour onto the dry ingredients and knead until you form a dough.

❖ Roll the dough out, about 5 mm (¼ inch) thick, onto two dehydrator trays lined with non-stick sheets. Score each into four even pieces using a sharp knife. (Alternatively, you can use a medium-sized bowl as a 'cookie cutter' to trim the bases into a more traditional round shape, instead of covering the dehydrator trays completely with dough.)

❖ Dehydrate for 12 hours at 40°C (105°F). Remove the non-stick sheets and dehydrate on mesh trays for a further 2–4 hours. Do not overdry them — the bases should still be a bit spongy in the middle. (If you don't have a dehydrator, place the rounds on baking trays lined with non-stick sheets and leave in the oven on its lowest setting, with the door slightly ajar, for 1 hour.)

❖ Once set, carefully cut along the scored lines using a sharp knife. Arrange in single layers in an airtight container, with baking paper between each layer. Store in the freezer for up to 4 weeks.

❖ To use, warm the pizza bases in the dehydrator for at least 20 minutes before serving.

ONION FLAT BREAD

MAKES 24 PIECES

This flat bread is an amazing base for sandwiches, and as a side for salads and soups. Make a huge batch and then freeze what you don't use, so you can have them on hand when your belly grumbles.

2½ large sweet yellow onions, thinly sliced (I use a mandoline for this)
165 g (5¾ oz/1½ cups) linseed (flaxseed) meal
150 g (5½ oz/1½ cups) sunflower seed meal

3 tablespoons tamari
125 ml (4 fl oz/½ cup) cold-pressed extra virgin olive oil
45 g (1½ oz/¼ cup) pitted medjool dates
60 g (2¼ oz/½ cup) raisins

✿ Combine the onion slices, linseed meal and sunflower seed meal in a large bowl.

✿ Mix the tamari, olive oil, dates and raisins in a high-speed blender until smooth, using a tamper to push the ingredients onto the blade, as the mixture will be very thick. Pour into the bowl, over the onion mixture, then mix well with your hands until you have a spreadable batter.

✿ Using a spatula, spread about 2½ cups of the mixture onto a dehydrator tray lined with a non-stick sheet. Score into 12 equal pieces. Repeat until all the batter is used; there should be enough for two standard dehydrator trays.

✿ Dehydrate at 40°C (105°F) for 12 hours. When the exposed side has set, flip each dough portion onto a mesh tray and peel off the non-stick sheets. Dehydrate for a further 6 hours, or until the breads are set, yet still pliable. (If you don't have a dehydrator, place the mixture on baking trays lined with non-stick sheets and leave in the oven on its lowest setting, with the door slightly ajar, for 2 hours, then flip and dehydrate for a further 30 minutes.)

✿ Cut each portion into 12 equal pieces, along the scored lines. Store in single layers in an airtight container, with baking paper between each layer. You can refrigerate what you will be using in the next few days, and freeze the rest in a snap-lock bag. The bread will keep in the freezer for up to 4 weeks.

BAGELS

MAKES 10 BAGELS

In New York City I found some amazing gluten-free bagels. I loved them so much, but they still made me feel a bit sluggish. When I came back home, I thought I'd try making a raw vegan version. And damn, it's good.

200 g (7 oz/2 cups) almond meal
130 g (4½ oz/1 cup) buckwheat flour (made by grinding activated buckwheat groats in a high-speed blender)
1 tablespoon garlic powder
1 teaspoon onion powder
1 teaspoon Himalayan pink salt or Celtic sea salt
40 g (1½ oz/½ cup) Irish moss gel; if unavailable, use 230 g (8 oz/½ cup) of puréed kelp noodles instead

25 g (1 oz/½ cup) peeled and roughly chopped carrots
90 g (3¼ oz/½ cup) pitted medjool dates
3 tablespoons lemon juice
3 tablespoons filtered alkaline water

Topping
3 tablespoons sesame seeds (white, black, or a mix of both)
3 tablespoons poppy seeds

❖ Combine the almond meal, buckwheat flour, garlic powder, onion powder and salt in a large mixing bowl.

❖ Blend the moss gel, carrot, dates, lemon juice and water in a high-speed blender until smooth. Pour onto the dry ingredients and knead until you form a dough.

❖ Divide into 10 equal portions and roll into uniformly sized balls. Flatten slightly, then use an apple corer or small round cookie cutter to cut out a centre hole, creating a bagel shape. Sprinkle the tops with the sesame seeds and poppy seeds.

❖ Place the bagels on mesh dehydrator trays and dehydrate for 12 hours at 40°C (105°F), or until the outside forms a crust, but the inside is still fluffy. (If you don't have a dehydrator, place the bagels on a baking tray and leave in the oven on its lowest setting, with the door slightly ajar, for 2 hours, then flip and dehydrate for a further 30 minutes.)

❖ The bagels will keep in an airtight container for 5 days, or can be frozen in a snap-lock bag for 4 weeks. To use, warm the bagels in the dehydrator for 20 minutes before serving.

BEET IT WRAPS

MAKES 12 WRAPS

Any time you feel a snack attack coming on, just roll these exquisitely pretty wraps around your favourite fillings and tell those hunger pangs to beet it.

325 g (11½ oz/4 cups) chopped young coconut flesh
3 tablespoons coconut water
3 tablespoons cold-pressed beetroot (beet) juice
1 teaspoon Himalayan pink salt or Celtic sea salt
50 g (1¾ oz/1 cup) shredded basil leaves

❖ Blend all the ingredients, except the basil leaves, in a high-speed blender until smooth. Toss in the shredded basil and mix by hand.
❖ Using a spatula, spread the mixture onto dehydrator trays lined with non-stick sheets. Score into four equal pieces. Repeat until all the batter is used; there should be enough for three standard dehydrator trays.
❖ Dehydrate at 40°C (105°F) for 6 hours. When the exposed side has set, flip each wrap onto a mesh tray and peel off the non-stick sheets. Dehydrate for a further 2 hours, or until the wraps are set, yet still pliable, taking care not to overdry them. (If you don't have a dehydrator, place the mixture on baking trays lined with non-stick sheets and leave in the oven on its lowest setting, with the door slightly ajar, for 30 minutes, then flip and dehydrate for a further 20 minutes, or until set but still pliable.)
❖ Cut each wrap into four equal pieces, along the scored lines. Store in single layers in an airtight container, with baking paper between each layer. You can refrigerate what you will be using in the next few days, and freeze the rest in a snap-lock bag for up to 4 weeks.

ZUCCHINI WRAPS

MAKES 12 WRAPS

Zucchini wraps are very versatile, and ideal for quick and easy lunches. I love rolling up some of my favourite salads in these, along with some Coconut bacon (page 128) or Eggplant pastrami (page 128) and a huge dollop of Tomato, paprika & zucchini hummus (page 125).

1.4 kg (3 lb 2 oz/8 cups) peeled and diced zucchini (courgettes); you'll need about 7 medium-sized ones
165 g (5¾ oz/1½ cups) linseed (flaxseed) meal
1 teaspoon Himalayan pink salt or Celtic sea salt

❖ Blend all the ingredients in a high-speed blender until smooth.
❖ Using a spatula, spread the mixture onto dehydrator trays lined with non-stick sheets. Score into four equal pieces. Repeat until all the batter is used; there should be enough for three standard dehydrator trays.
❖ Dehydrate at 40°C (105°F) for 6 hours. When the exposed side has set, flip each wrap onto a mesh tray and peel off the non-stick sheets. Dehydrate for a further 2 hours, or until the wraps are set, yet still pliable, taking care not to overdry them. (If you don't have a dehydrator, place the mixture on baking trays lined with non-stick sheets and leave in the oven on its lowest setting, with the door slightly ajar, for 30 minutes, then flip and dehydrate for a further 20 minutes, or until set but still pliable.)
❖ Cut each wrap into four equal pieces, along the scored lines. Store in single layers in an airtight container, with baking paper between each layer. You can refrigerate what you will be using in the next few days, and freeze the rest in a snap-lock bag for up to 4 weeks.

ZUCCHINI CRACKERS

SERVES 4

These crackers happen to be in a rather delicious open relationship with the Brazil nut cheddar cream cheeze (page 79).

4–6 sun-dried tomatoes
3 zucchini (courgettes), chopped
150 g (5½ oz/1½ cups) activated walnuts
155 g (5½ oz/1 cup) activated almonds
55 g (2 oz/½ cup) activated linseeds (flaxseeds), ground
3 tablespoons hemp seeds
½ red capsicum (pepper), seeded and chopped
juice of 1 lemon
2 heaped tablespoons nutritional yeast
1 teaspoon Himalayan pink salt or Celtic sea salt
2 tablespoons filtered alkaline water

❧ Soak the sun-dried tomatoes in filtered alkaline water for 1 hour to soften them.
❧ Drain the tomatoes, then place in a food processor. Add the remaining ingredients, slowly adding the water until a sticky dough forms.
❧ Spread the dough on dehydrator trays lined with non-stick sheets. Use a sharp knife to score the dough into the shape and size of cracker that you prefer. Dehydrate at 40°C (105°F) for 8 hours, flipping them over and removing the non-stick sheets after 4 hours, or when the exposed side is firm. (If you don't have a dehydrator, place the mixture on baking trays lined with non-stick sheets and leave in the oven on its lowest setting, with the door slightly ajar, for 2 hours, then flip and dehydrate for a further 1 hour.)
❧ Cut the crackers to shape by cutting along the scored lines. Store in single layers in an airtight container, with baking paper between each layer. The crackers will keep at room temperature for 5 days, or in the freezer for up to 4 weeks. If using from the freezer, warm the crackers in the dehydrator for 20 minutes before serving.

COCONUT WRAPS

MAKES 12 WRAPS

You can enjoy these wraps with fillings savoury or sweet. Try adding some coconut nectar to the mix, and using the wraps to make desserts; my favourite combo is banana, dates and peanut butter inside a sweet coconut wrap.

325 g (11½ oz/4 cups) chopped young coconut flesh
125 ml (4 fl oz/½ cup) coconut water
1 teaspoon Himalayan pink salt or Celtic sea salt

For sweet coconut wraps
4 tablespoons coconut nectar

❧ Blend all the ingredients in a high-speed blender until smooth.
❧ Using a spatula, spread the mixture onto dehydrator trays lined with non-stick sheets. Score into four equal pieces. Repeat until all the batter is used; there should be enough for three standard dehydrator trays.
❧ Dehydrate at 40°C (105°F) for 6 hours. When the exposed side has set, flip the each wrap onto a mesh tray and peel off the non-stick sheets. Dehydrate for a further 2 hours, or until the wraps are set, yet still pliable, taking care not to overdry them. (If you don't have a dehydrator, place the mixture on baking trays lined with non-stick sheets and leave in the oven on its lowest setting, with the door slightly ajar, for 30 minutes, then flip and dehydrate for a further 20 minutes, or until set but still pliable.)
❧ Cut each wrap into four equal pieces, along the scored lines. Store in single layers in an airtight container, with baking paper between each layer. You can refrigerate what you will be using in the next few days, and freeze the rest in a snap-lock bag for up to 4 weeks.

GARLIC & HERB BREAD

MAKES 8 SMALL LOAVES

The perfect accompaniment for raw zucchini (courgette) pastas
(see pages 88, 94, 95, 100 and 104), these babies are also pretty
marvellous slathered with Aged macadamia cheeze (page 79).

200 g (7 oz/2 cups) almond meal
80 g (2¾ oz/1 cup) psyllium husks
55 g (2 oz/½ cup) linseed
   (flaxseed) meal
1½ teaspoons Himalayan pink salt
   or Celtic sea salt
2 teaspoons dried oregano
2 teaspoons dried thyme
2 teaspoons dried basil

60 g (2¼ oz/½ cup) chopped
   garlic chives
235 g (8½ oz/1½ cups) chopped
   white onion
4 garlic cloves, peeled
3 teaspoons lemon juice
80 ml (2½ fl oz/⅓ cup) filtered
   alkaline water

❖ Combine the almond meal, psyllium, linseed meal, salt and dried herbs
in a large mixing bowl.
❖ In a food processor, blend the garlic chives, onion, garlic and lemon
juice to a paste. Add the paste to the dry ingredients, along with the
water, then knead until you form a dough.
❖ Shape into eight small loaves, then place on mesh dehydrator trays.
Dehydrate for 12 hours at 40°C (105°F), or until the outside forms a crust,
but the inside remains fluffy. (If you don't have a dehydrator, place the
loaves on baking trays and leave in the oven on its lowest setting, with
the door slightly ajar, for 2 hours.)
❖ The loaves will keep in airtight containers for 5 days, or can be frozen
in snap-lock bags for up to 4 weeks.

BURGER BUNS

MAKES 12

When you're out to impress, dish out a round of raw sliders in these adorable little buns. Because everything is cuter fun-sized, right?

400 g (14 oz/4 cups) almond meal
80 g (2¾ oz/1 cup) psyllium husks
110 g (3¾ oz/1 cup) linseed (flaxseed) meal
90 g (3¼ oz/½ cup) pitted medjool dates
2 tablespoons lemon juice
2 teaspoons Himalayan pink salt

1 tablespoon dried parsley
2 teaspoons dried dill or sage
375 ml (13 fl oz/1½ cups) filtered alkaline water

Topping
3 tablespoons mixed black and white sesame seeds

❖ Combine the almond meal, psyllium and linseed meal in a large mixing bowl.
❖ Blend the dates, lemon juice, salt, herbs and half the water in a high-speed blender, until a paste forms. Add the paste and the remaining water to the dry ingredients and knead until you form a dough.
❖ On a clean surface, roll the dough out to about 1 cm (½ inch) thick. Use a small glass or cookie cutter to cut out 12 rounds from the dough. Form the rounds into burger buns, then sprinkle with the sesame seeds.
❖ Place the buns on mesh dehydrator trays and dehydrate for 12 hours at 40°C (105°F). (If you don't have a dehydrator, place the buns on baking trays and leave in the oven on its lowest setting, with the door slightly ajar, for 2 hours.) Do not overdry the buns, or they will turn into cookies.
❖ Once done, arrange the buns in single layers inside airtight containers, with baking paper between each layer. Store in the freezer; the buns will keep for up to 4 weeks. To use, warm the buns in the dehydrator for at least 30 minutes before serving.

SADHANA KITCHEN
SUPER BOWL

CAESAR SALAD WITH ZUCHOVY

SERVES 4

At Sadhana Kitchen, when we spiralise zucchini to make our Zoodles (page 70)
or zucchini 'pastas', we use the left-over zucchini cores to make a dried 'zucchini
anchovy' — or 'zuchovy', as we like to call it — to sprinkle over our caesar salads.
(The 'anchovy' component is actually dulse, a red seaweed that tastes of the sea.)
This amazing salad is creamy, filling and a meal in its own right. If you know anyone
who doesn't eat salad, give them this and they might just change their mind.

Zuchovy
130 g (4½ oz/1 cup) zucchini
(courgette) cores, left-over after
spiralising zucchini, chopped into
5 cm (2 inch) pieces
1 tablespoon cold-pressed extra
virgin olive oil
1 tablespoon caper brine
1 tablespoon dill tips
1 teaspoon dulse flakes
1 teaspoon Himalayan pink salt
or Celtic sea salt

Dressing
80 g (2¾ oz/½ cup) activated
cashew nuts
3 tablespoons pine nuts
4 tablespoons lemon juice
2 garlic cloves, peeled
2 teaspoons brown rice miso paste
½ teaspoon dulse flakes
2 tablespoons chopped dill
2 large medjool dates, pitted
½ teaspoon freshly ground
black pepper
250 ml (9 fl oz/1 cup) filtered
alkaline water

Salad
200 g (7 oz/4 cups) shredded cos
(romaine) lettuce
140 g (5 oz/2 cups) shredded kale

To serve
3 tablespoons pine nuts

❖ Toss all the zuchovy ingredients together in a bowl
and leave to marinate for 20 minutes.

❖ Place the zuchovy ingredients on a dehydrator tray
lined with a non-stick sheet and dehydrate at 40°C
(105°F) for 4 hours. (If you don't have a dehydrator,
place the zuchovy on a baking tray lined with a
non-stick sheet and leave in the oven on its lowest
setting, with the door slightly ajar, for 15 minutes.)

❖ When the zuchovy is done, blend all the dressing
ingredients in a high-speed blender until smooth.
Pour into a large mixing bowl. Add the lettuce and
kale and massage together until thoroughly covered
with the dressing.

❖ Divide the mixture among four bowls. Top with the
zuchovy and pine nuts and serve.

 TIP   A spiraliser is a handy kitchen gadget that cuts
fruit and vegetables into long 'noodles' or pasta
shapes. Depending on the blades you attach, your
pasta can be tubular like spaghetti, or flat like
fettuccine. They are fairly inexpensive and great
for achieving a variety of textures in your dishes,
making raw pasta and noodle dishes very quick
and easy to prepare.

FERMENTS

A HEALTHY DOSE OF CULTURE

For centuries, fermented foods have played an important role in traditional diets the world over, both as a method of preserving food throughout the leaner months, and for their many nutritional benefits. Fermented foods such as Kimchi (page 83) and Sauerkraut (page 84) are rich in beneficial probiotic bacteria and yeasts, which can help support digestive processes, improve resistance to allergies, boost immunity, enhance metabolism and manage sugar cravings. The best part — aside from how very tasty fermented foods can be! — is that they are very easy and inexpensive to prepare at home.

SOUR CREAM

**MAKES 500 G
(1 LB 2 OZ/2 CUPS)**

This simple recipe can be added to any meal for that extra creaminess. If you're short on time, you don't have to ferment the mixture, but it's so much better for you if you do.

310 g (11 oz/2 cups) activated cashew nuts
1 teaspoon probiotic powder
435 ml (15 fl oz/1¾ cups) filtered alkaline water
juice of 1 lemon
¼ teaspoon Himalayan pink salt
1 tablespoon apple cider vinegar
2 tablespoons nutritional yeast

❖ Blend the cashews, probiotic powder and water in a high-speed blender until smooth.
❖ Transfer to a glass jar, cover with muslin (cheesecloth) and secure with a rubber band. Leave to ferment in a warm place for 24 hours.
❖ Once fermented, place back into the blender jug, along with the remaining ingredients. Blend on high speed until well combined, adding small amounts of extra water at a time if the mixture is too thick, until the desired consistency is reached.
❖ Pour into a clean, airtight glass jar and seal the lid.
❖ The sour cream will keep in the fridge for 7 days, and will continue to ferment slowly.

COCONUT YOGHURT

SERVES 4

Coconut yoghurt can be quite pricey when buying it ready-made from a store. Luckily, it's quick and easy to make at home. You can add just about anything to this and use it for sweet or savoury applications. It goes deliciously well with chopped cucumber and mint to make a raita, and some Raspberry chia jam (page 148) for a sweet berry twist.

320 g (11½ oz/2 cups) chopped coconut flesh
250 ml (9 fl oz/1 cup) coconut water
1 teaspoon probiotic powder

❖ Blend all the ingredients in a high-speed blender until smooth.
❖ Transfer to a glass jar, cover with muslin (cheesecloth) and secure with a rubber band. Leave at room temperature for 24 hours.
❖ When it is ready, the yoghurt should taste tangy. You can then add flavourings to make sweet or savoury variations.
❖ The yoghurt will keep in an airtight container in the fridge for 7 days, and will continue to ferment slowly.

AGED MACADAMIA CHEEZE

SERVES 4

I used to sit down and eat a whole wheel of camembert cheese watching telly. I never thought I could live without cheese, but it turns out you don't have to. This recipe is a great alternative for dairy cheese, minus the animal cruelty. It's also a great base to add your own flair to. Roll it in cracked pepper, add any herbs and flavouring you like and you've got yourself your very own cheezy creation.

310 g (11 oz/2 cups) activated macadamia nuts
1 teaspoon probiotic powder
¼ teaspoon Himalayan pink salt
2 tablespoons nutritional yeast
310 ml (10¾ fl oz/1¼ cups) filtered alkaline water

❧ Blend all the ingredients in a high-speed blender until smooth, using a tamper to push the mixture onto the blades, as it will be very thick.
❧ Line a fine-meshed sieve with muslin (cheesecloth), then place it over a bowl, to catch the whey during the fermentation process. Pour the cheeze mixture into the sieve.
❧ Fold the excess cheesecloth in on itself, so it covers the top of the cheeze. Place some nuts or seeds in a glass jar and use it as a weight to gently press on top of the cheesecloth. Leave to ferment in a warm place for 24 hours.
❧ Once fermented, transfer to a 10 cm (4 inch) round spring-form tin lined with plastic wrap. (You can save the nutritious whey to add to your smoothies.)
❧ Place the tin of cheeze into the freezer to firm up for about 1 hour.
❧ Remove the cheeze wheel from the tin and place on a dehydrator tray.
❧ Dehydrate at 40°C (105°F) for 12 hours, or until a 'skin' forms on the outside. (If you don't have a dehydrator, place the cheeze on a baking tray and leave in the oven on its lowest setting, with the door slightly ajar, for 2 hours.)
❧ The cheeze will keep in an airtight container in the fridge for 7 days, and will continue to ferment slowly.

BRAZIL NUT CHEDDAR CREAM CHEEZE

MAKES 500 G
(1 LB 2 OZ/2 CUPS)

This spreadable cream cheeze is great on raw crackers and served alongside any salad. As with the sour cream, you don't have to ferment the mixture if you don't have time, but then you miss out on all the awesome healthy bacteria for your belly.

155 g (5½ oz/1 cup) activated Brazil nuts
155 g (5½ oz/1 cup) activated cashew nuts
1 teaspoon probiotic powder
3 garlic cloves, peeled
½ red or yellow capsicum (pepper), seeded and chopped
juice of ½ lemon
3 tablespoons apple cider vinegar
3 tablespoons nutritional yeast
Himalayan pink salt or Celtic sea salt, to taste
3 tablespoons filtered alkaline water

❧ Blend the Brazil nuts, cashews, probiotic powder and water in a high-speed blender until smooth.
❧ Transfer to a glass jar, cover with muslin (cheesecloth) and secure with a rubber band. Leave to ferment in a warm place for 24 hours.
❧ Once fermented, place back into the blender jug, along with the remaining ingredients. Blend on high speed until well combined, adding small amounts of extra water at a time if the mixture is too thick, until the desired consistency is reached.
❧ Pour into a clean, airtight glass jar and seal the lid.
❧ The cheeze will keep in the fridge for 7 days, and will continue to ferment slowly.

HERBED PINE NUT & CASHEW CHEEZE LOG

SERVES 4

So damn delicious, this cheeze log goes especially well with Bagels (page 60) and Garlic & herb bread (page 64). And just about everything, really!

155 g (5½ oz/1 cup) activated cashew nuts
155 g (5½ oz/1 cup) pine nuts
1 teaspoon probiotic powder
¼ teaspoon Himalayan pink salt
2 tablespoons nutritional yeast
310 ml (10¾ fl oz/1¼ cups) filtered alkaline water
2 tablespoons chopped dill
4 tablespoons chopped chives
½ teaspoon freshly cracked black pepper

❖ Blend all the ingredients, except the herbs and cracked pepper, in a high-speed blender until smooth, using a tamper to push the mixture onto the blades, as it will be very thick.
❖ Line a fine-meshed sieve with muslin (cheesecloth), then place over a bowl, to catch the whey during the fermentation process. Pour the cheeze mixture into the sieve.
❖ Fold the excess cheesecloth in on itself, so it covers the top of the cheeze. Place some nuts or seeds in a glass jar and use it as a weight to gently press on top of the cheesecloth. Leave to ferment in a warm place for 24 hours.
❖ Once fermented, transfer to a sheet of plastic wrap, stretched across a flat surface. Mould into a log, then roll the cheeze in the plastic wrap, forming a sausage shape, twisting the ends to secure it in place. Leave in the fridge to firm up for about 2 hours.
❖ Spread the herbs and pepper evenly over a chopping board. Remove the cheeze log from the fridge and unwrap.
❖ Roll the cheeze in the herb mixture and wrap in a new piece of plastic wrap. Set in the fridge for a further 1 hour before serving.
❖ The cheeze will keep in the fridge for 7 days, and will continue to ferment slowly.

PICKLED GINGER

SERVES 4

I can't get enough of this stuff with my seaweed salads or raw vegan sushi rolls. Make a huge batch and keep it in the fridge so you can add this pickled deliciousness to your meals at will.

400 g (14 oz/2 cups) peeled and finely sliced fresh ginger (I use a mandoline for this)
250 ml (9 fl oz/1 cup) apple cider vinegar
2 tablespoons coconut nectar

❖ Combine all the ingredients in a bowl and massage together well. Transfer to a clean, airtight glass jar and leave to ferment at room temperature for 3–4 days.
❖ Store in the fridge once fermented to your liking. The pickled ginger will keep for a few weeks.

KOMBUCHA

MAKES 3.5 LITRES (122 FL OZ/14 CUPS)

Consumed for centuries for its health benefits, kombucha is a probiotic-rich fermented tea. To make it, you'll need a 'scoby' — the bacterial colony responsible for the fermentation process. It looks like a glutinous rice pancake or jellyfish and can be purchased online, or if you know someone who makes their own kombucha, they might donate you one. Scobies grow to the size of the vessel you are fermenting your kombucha in. The 'mother' scoby gives birth to a 'baby' scoby each cycle. You can harvest these babies and store them in a sterilised glass jar in their own juices, or share the scobies with your mates.

Use this base recipe to ferment the kombucha. You can then add fresh fruit, cold-pressed juices or herbs, along with some ice, to make the most delicious iced drinks.

3.5 litres (122 fl oz/14 cups) filtered alkaline water
3 tablespoons of your favourite loose-leaf black, green or white tea leaves; make sure the tea doesn't contain any oils or added flavourings
200 g (7 oz/1 cup) organic cane juice crystals (also sold as rapadura sugar)
250 ml (9 fl oz/1 cup) store-bought kombucha tea
1 scoby

❖ Bring the water to the boil in a large saucepan. Add the tea leaves and sugar. Brew for 4–5 minutes, or until the desired strength is reached. Take off the heat and cool to room temperature.
❖ Meanwhile, sterilise a large glass vessel. Add the cooled tea, kombucha starter and scoby. Cover the mouth of the vessel with a clean cloth and secure with a rubber band or twine.
❖ Place in a safe area where it will not be moved or disturbed, away from direct sunlight. Leave to ferment for 5–8 days. Check the pH level using pH strips (which you can buy inexpensively from health-food stores or online). The pH should register between 2.7 and 3.2 when the tea is ready. (Once you've made a few batches, you can smell and taste when the kombucha is ready.)
❖ Bottle the tea and reserve 250 ml (9 fl oz/1 cup) for starting off your next batch. Enjoy chilled.

KIMCHI

SERVES 4

Store-bought kimchi usually contains fish sauce. With this recipe you can keep it vegan, and make it as hot or mild as you like. Add some to your salads for extra kick.

300 g (10½ oz/4 cups) roughly chopped savoy cabbage
200 g (7 oz/1 cup) grated apple
80 g (2¾ oz/½ cup) grated carrot
45 g (1½ oz/½ cup) grated daikon
30 g (1 oz/½ cup) chopped spring onion (scallion)
4 cm (1½ inch) knob of fresh ginger, peeled and finely grated
2 garlic cloves, crushed
3 tablespoons Korean red chilli powder (gochugaru)
2 teaspoons Himalayan pink salt or Celtic sea salt
2 teaspoons probiotic powder
4 large cabbage leaves, for sealing the jar

❖ Combine all the ingredients, except the whole cabbage leaves, in a mixing bowl, thoroughly massaging the spices into the shredded cabbage and apple.
❖ Pack tightly into a sterilised glass jar. Roll the cabbage leaves up and use them to seal the top of the jar, before securing the lid on.
❖ Leave to ferment at room temperature for 24–48 hours, 'burping' your kimchi every day by opening the lid and allowing the gasses to escape.
❖ Store in the refrigerator once cultured. The kimchi will keep for a few weeks, and will continue to ferment slowly.

PICKLED VEGETABLES

SERVES 4

I try to eat about half a cup of fermented food each day for a healthy dose of probiotics. These pickled vegies, as well as being exquisitely pretty, make a delicious addition to any main meal.

45 g (1½ oz/½ cup) julienned carrot
75 g (2½ oz/½ cup) julienned beetroot (beet)
100 g (3½ oz/½ cup) grated apple
125 g (4½ oz/1 cup) cauliflower florets (as small as possible)
2 teaspoons Himalayan pink salt or Celtic sea salt
1 teaspoon caraway seeds
1 tablespoon chopped dill
4 tablespoons coconut nectar
1 teaspoon probiotic powder

❖ Combine all the ingredients in a bowl and massage together well; the salt will draw out moisture from the vegies.
❖ Transfer to a clean, airtight glass jar, making sure the natural moisture covers all the vegies. If it doesn't, add some salted water, made to a ratio of 1 tablespoon Himalayan pink salt or Celtic sea salt to 500 ml (17 fl oz/2 cups) filtered alkaline water.
❖ Seal the jar and leave to ferment at room temperature for 3–4 days.
❖ Store in the fridge once fermented to your liking. The pickled vegies will keep for a few weeks.

SAUERKRAUT

SERVES 4

Eating fermented foods every day is a wonderful and tasty way of aiding the body's natural detoxification processes. This sauerkraut is one of my regular meal accompaniments. Munch on a small portion every day and glow from the inside out.

300 g (10½ oz/4 cups) shredded red cabbage
200 g (7 oz/1 cup) grated apple
1 tablespoon whole cloves
1 tablespoon freshly ground black pepper
4 garlic cloves, crushed
1 teaspoon cumin seeds
1 tablespoon crushed bay leaves
2 teaspoons Himalayan pink salt or Celtic sea salt
2 teaspoons probiotic powder
4 large cabbage leaves, for sealing the jar

❖ Combine all the ingredients, except the whole cabbage leaves, in a mixing bowl, thoroughly massaging the spices into the shredded cabbage and apple.
❖ Pack tightly into a sterilised, airtight glass jar. Roll the cabbage leaves up and use them to seal the top of the jar, before securing the lid on.
❖ Leave to ferment at room temperature for 24–48 hours, 'burping' your sauerkraut every day by opening the lid and allowing the gasses to escape.
❖ Store in the refrigerator once cultured. The sauerkraut will keep for a few weeks, and will continue to ferment slowly.

1 PICKLED VEGETABLES
2 SAUERKRAUT

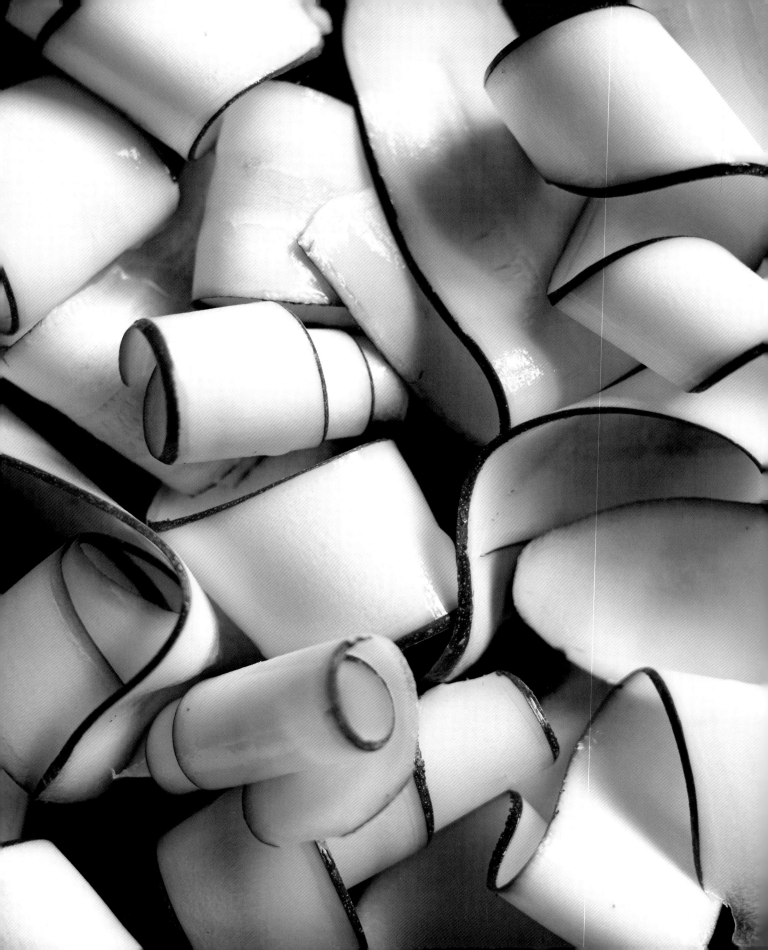

FALAFEL PLATE WITH BEETROOT DIP & ZUCCHINI HUMMUS

SERVES 4

Hands up if you've been out on the town, drunk as hell and hungry enough to eat your weight in kebabs? I know I have. This falafel plate is a much sexier, less messy and less drunken version of that kebab. If you want it to be even closer to the original experience, you can pop the components in a wrap and eat it outside a club at 3 am, with some guy passed out in the gutter next to you.

Falafels

4 large carrots, peeled and chopped
155 g (5½ oz/1 cup) activated almonds
25 g (1 oz/¼ cup) activated walnuts
3 tablespoons activated sunflower seeds
3 tablespoons nutritional yeast
3 garlic cloves, peeled
1 tablespoon ground cumin

¼ teaspoon chipotle chilli powder
1½ teaspoons Himalayan pink salt or Celtic sea salt
3 tablespoons white sesame seeds
2 tablespoons black sesame seeds
2 tablespoons tahini
2 tablespoons lemon juice

To serve

250 g (9 oz/4 cups) baby salad leaves
1 batch Pickled vegetables (page 84)
1 batch Beetroot dip (page 122)
1 batch Tomato, paprika & zucchini hummus (page 125)
1 batch Garlic sauce (page 118), in a squeeze bottle
4 tablespoons black sesame seeds

❖ To make the falafels, blend the carrots in a food processor until very finely chopped, then transfer to a large mixing bowl. To the food processor, add the almonds, walnuts, sunflower seeds, yeast, garlic, cumin, chilli powder and salt. Blend until well combined, then add to the chopped carrot and mix well using your hands. Now add the white and black sesame seeds, tahini and lemon juice and fold together.

❖ Using an ice cream scoop, shape the mixture into falafel balls. Place on mesh dehydrator trays and dehydrate at 40°C (105°F) for 8 hours, or until crispy on the outside, but moist and juicy on the inside. (If you don't have a dehydrator, place the falafel balls on a baking tray and leave in the oven on its lowest setting, with the door slightly ajar, for 1 hour.)

❖ To serve, pop four falafels on each plate, along with 1 cup of baby salad leaves. Add some pickled vegetables, a dollop of the beetroot dip and a dollop of the hummus.

❖ Squeeze little mounds of garlic sauce onto the falafels, then sprinkle with the black sesame seeds. Pretend it's 3 am and you've just had a huge night clubbing. Devour with gusto.

BASIL PESTO FETTUCCINI

SERVES 4

Raw pastas are a great dinner option because they are so quick and easy to make, and are marvellously tasty too. You can add as many vegies as you like, taking their nutritional content to the next level.

8 large zucchini (courgettes)
3 tablespoons pine nuts

Basil, kale & pine nut pesto
75 g (2½ oz/1½ cups, tightly packed) basil leaves
85 g (3 oz/1 cup, tightly packed) chopped kale
310 g (11 oz/2 cups) pine nuts
500 ml (17 fl oz/2 cups) cold-pressed extra virgin olive oil
4 garlic cloves, peeled
3 tablespoons lemon juice
1 teaspoon Himalayan pink salt or Celtic sea salt

❖ To prepare the 'pasta', peel the zucchini, then use a mandoline or vegetable peeler to shave the zucchini into fettuccini strips. Place in a large mixing bowl.
❖ Pulse all the pesto ingredients in a food processor until well combined, but still chunky. Add the pesto to the zucchini pasta and massage it in well.
❖ Divide among four serving bowls and top with pine nuts.

OYSTER MUSHROOM LO MEIN

SERVES 4

I love a good noodle dish. This one is so quick, simple and super tasty. And the best thing is that you can use whatever vegetables are in season, or the ones you love best.

2 x 340 g (12 oz) packets of kelp noodles
60 g (2¼ oz/1 cup) broccoli florets
90 g (3¼ oz/1 cup) julienned carrot
45 g (1½ oz/1 cup) shredded Chinese cabbage (wong bok)
100 g (3½ oz) snow peas (mangetout)
200 g (7 oz) oyster mushrooms, sliced
115 g (4 oz/1 cup) bean sprouts
chilli flakes, for sprinkling

Lemon & sesame marinade
3 tablespoons Kecap manis (page 119)
juice of 1 lemon
2 teaspoons cold-pressed sesame oil
2 garlic cloves, crushed

❖ Soak the kelp noodles in filtered alkaline water while making the marinade.
❖ Blend the marinade ingredients, along with a dose of good vibes, in a high-speed blender until well combined. Pour into a large mixing bowl. Add the broccoli, carrot, cabbage, snow peas and mushrooms and toss together.
❖ Drain the noodles and gently mix them through the vegetables, then leave to marinate for 20 minutes.
❖ Divide the mixture among four bowls. Finish with the bean sprouts and a sprinkling of chilli flakes.

SPAGHETTI & BEET BALLS

> SERVES 4

Here's another good one for the kids, because they love getting in on the action and rolling those vegie balls. If you're serving it to little ones, you can leave out the chilli.

8 large zucchini (courgettes), peeled and spiralised (see Tip on page 72), or shaved into fettuccini strips

3 tablespoons roughly chopped flat-leaf (Italian) parsley

Beet balls

1 small beetroot (beet), peeled and diced

90 g (3¼ oz/1 cup) sliced shiitake mushrooms, finely chopped using a food processor

1 carrot, peeled and roughly chopped, then finely chopped using a food processor

100 g (3½ oz/¾ cup) finely diced celery

220 g (7¾ oz/1½ cups) activated sunflower seeds, finely ground using a food processor

3 tablespoons linseed (flaxseed) meal

4 tablespoons tamari

1 tablespoon onion powder

1 teaspoon dried thyme

1 teaspoon dried sage

1 teaspoon dried rosemary

¼ teaspoon freshly ground black pepper

Marinara sauce

75 g (2½ oz/½ cup) sun-dried tomatoes, soaked in filtered alkaline water for 1 hour, then drained

3 garlic cloves, peeled

600 g (1 lb 5 oz/3 cups) chopped, seeded tomatoes

1½ tablespoons fresh oregano

125 ml (4 fl oz/½ cup) cold-pressed extra virgin olive oil

3 tablespoons lemon juice

2 tablespoons coconut nectar

pinch of Himalayan pink salt or Celtic sea salt

¼ teaspoon freshly ground black pepper

½ teaspoon chilli flakes

✿ Toss all the beet balls ingredients together in a mixing bowl until well combined. Roll into uniform-sized balls.

✿ Place on mesh dehydrator trays and dehydrate at 40°C (105°F) for 4 hours, or until crispy on the outside, but moist and juicy on the inside. The beet balls will darken as you dehydrate them, and this is completely normal. (If you don't have a dehydrator, place the beet balls on baking trays and leave in the oven on its lowest setting, with the door slightly ajar, for 1 hour.)

✿ Once the beet balls are done, pop them into a mixing bowl. Place all the marinara sauce ingredients in a high-speed blender and blend until smooth, then pour over the beet balls.

✿ Divide the zucchini pasta among four serving bowls, then top with the beet balls and marinara sauce. Finish with the parsley and serve.

CHIPOTLE MUSHROOM BURGERS WITH THE LOT

SERVES 4

Raw food can sometimes be super-rich and dense. In such cases, it's better to make smaller serving sizes, because that's all you really need. So, these burgers are more like sliders in their size, but one will do the trick in satisfying your hunger and nutritional needs.

Mushroom patties
100 g (3½ oz) shiitake mushrooms, chopped
1 small carrot, peeled and chopped
30 g (1 oz/¼ cup) chopped celery
50 g (1¾ oz/½ cup) activated walnuts
1 garlic clove, peeled
4 tablespoons finely chopped coriander (cilantro)
3 tablespoons linseed (flaxseed) meal

1 teaspoon tamari
1 teaspoon lemon juice
1 teaspoon chipotle chilli powder
3 teaspoons onion powder
1 teaspoon smoked paprika

Caramelised onion
2 large onions, sliced into 5 mm (¼ inch) rings
3 tablespoons tamari
3 tablespoons coconut nectar

To serve
4 Burger buns (page 65), cut in half
1 batch Tomato sauce (page 114), in a squeeze bottle
50 g (1¾ oz/1 cup) shredded cos (romaine) lettuce
1 tomato, sliced

❖ To make the mushroom patties, combine the carrot, celery, walnuts, garlic and coriander in a food processor and blend until well combined. Transfer to a large mixing bowl. Add the remaining patty ingredients and knead until well combined. Shape into four patties the same size as your burger buns.
❖ Place on dehydrator trays lined with non-stick sheets. Dehydrate for 6 hours at 40°C (105°F). Remove the non-stick sheets, flip the patties over and dehydrate on mesh trays for a further 2–4 hours. (If you don't have a dehydrator, place the patties on baking trays lined with non-stick sheets and leave in the oven on its lowest setting, with the door slightly ajar, for 45 minutes, then flip them over and dehydrate for a further 10 minutes.)

❖ Combine the caramelised onion ingredients in a small bowl and leave to marinate for 20 minutes. Place on dehydrator trays lined with non-stick sheets and dehydrate for 4 hours at 40°C (105°F). (If you don't have a dehydrator, place the onion on a lined baking tray and leave in the oven on its lowest setting, with the door slightly ajar, for 25 minutes.) The caramelised onion can be made up to 5 days ahead and stored in an airtight container in the fridge.
❖ To assemble the burgers, take the bottom half of each burger bun and squeeze some tomato sauce on top. Top each one with lettuce, a tomato slice, one mushroom patty and some caramelised onion.
❖ Add another drizzle of tomato sauce, then pop the bun lids on top and serve.

BANH MI WRAPS
WITH SRIRACHA MAYO

SERVES 4

Bursting with flavour and freshness, the traditional Vietnamese *banh mi* is my ultimate sandwich, but the bread rolls they are usually served in — and some of the processed ingredients they can contain — make me feel tired and sluggish. This raw vegan version has similar flavours, without the need to nap after you eat it.

Filling
90 g (3¼ oz/1 cup) julienned carrot
2 tablespoons coconut nectar
2 tablespoons apple cider vinegar
50 g (1¾ oz/1 cup) shredded cos
   (romaine) lettuce
115 g (4 oz/1 cup) bean sprouts
15 g (½ oz/½ cup) coriander
   (cilantro) leaves

To serve
4 Coconut wraps (page 63)
1 batch Kecap manis (page 119),
   in a squeeze bottle
1 batch Coconut bacon (page 128)
sliced long red chilli (optional)
1 batch Sriracha mayo (page 121),
   in a squeeze bottle
lime wedges

❖ Start by pickling the carrot for the filling. In a small bowl, toss together the carrot, coconut nectar and vinegar. Cover and leave to marinate for 1 hour.

❖ To assemble, place one coconut wrap on a clean, flat surface. Squeeze some kecap manis all over it. Right in the middle of the wrap, stack thin rows of lettuce, coconut bacon, pickled carrot, bean sprouts and coriander. Add some chilli slices if desired.

❖ Squeeze some sriracha mayo on top, then roll up the wrap.

❖ Repeat with the remaining wraps and ingredients. Serve with lime wedges for squeezing over the top.

PASTA PUTTANESCA

SERVES 4

This dish is chunky and spicy and oh so satisfying. The heat from the chilli is a great way to warm the body when you're feeling cold, without having to physically heat the temperature of the food. Incidentally, while the origins of this pasta dish are debatable, the name literally translates to 'pasta of the whore' — so it's spicy in more ways than one.

8 large zucchini (courgettes)
4 tablespoons capers (reserve 1 tablespoon of the brine for the Puttanesca sauce)
75 g (2½ oz/½ cup) pitted kalamata olive halves
3 tablespoons shredded basil
3 tablespoons roughly chopped curly parsley, plus extra to serve
chilli flakes, to serve
1 tablespoon cold-pressed extra virgin olive oil, for drizzling

Puttanesca sauce
75 g (2½ oz/½ cup) sun-dried tomatoes, soaked in filtered alkaline water for 1 hour, then drained (see Tip)
3 garlic cloves, peeled
600 g (1 lb 5 oz/3 cups) seeded and chopped tomatoes
40 g (1½ oz/¼ cup) diced white onion
3 tablespoons cold-pressed extra virgin olive oil
½ teaspoon Himalayan pink salt or Celtic sea salt
1 teaspoon chilli flakes
½ teaspoon freshly ground black pepper
1 tablespoon caper brine

❖ To prepare the zucchini pasta, peel the zucchini, then use a mandoline or vegetable peeler to shave the zucchini into fettuccini strips. Place in a large mixing bowl.
❖ Combine all the puttanesca sauce ingredients in a high-speed blender until smooth. Stir in the capers, olives, basil and parsley.
❖ Divide the zucchini pasta among four serving bowls, then top with the puttanesca sauce. Finish with some extra parsley, a sprinkling of chilli flakes and a drizzle of olive oil.

 TIP You can reserve the tomato soaking water for extra flavour in vegetable stocks and sauces.

NOT-REALLY-TUNA SANDWICH

SERVES 4

We sometimes have this dude on special at Sadhana Kitchen, and it's always really popular. It tastes so much like the tuna mayo sandwiches my dad used to make for my school lunches, but is 100% fish friendly — all the love and taste, but none of the yucky bits.

Not-really-tuna

80 g (2¾ oz/½ cup) activated almonds

75 g (2½ oz/½ cup) activated sunflower seeds

3 tablespoons filtered alkaline water

35 g (1¼ oz/¼ cup) finely diced celery

3 tablespoons finely chopped dill pickles

40 g (1½ oz/¼ cup) finely chopped red onion

3 tablespoons finely chopped curly parsley

3 tablespoons lemon juice

2 teaspoons dulse flakes

½ teaspoon black salt

1 tablespoon chopped dill

To serve

8 pieces of Onion flat bread (page 59)

2 tomatoes, sliced

3 tablespoons finely chopped dill pickles

60 g (2¼ oz/1 cup) alfalfa sprouts

❖ To make the not-really-tuna, place the almonds, sunflower seeds and water in a high-speed blender. Using a tamper, push the ingredients onto the blade on high speed until a thick paste forms. Transfer to a bowl, add the remaining not-really-tuna ingredients and combine well using a fork.

❖ To assemble, spread four pieces of the onion flat bread with a generous amount of not-really-tuna. Top each with two tomato slices, some pickles and alfalfa sprouts.

❖ Place the remaining flat breads on top and serve.

MUSHROOM FIESTA TACOS WITH CHIMICHURRI

SERVES 4

Apart from cakes, this recipe is the one I serve up for people who are a little dubious about trying raw food. It hasn't failed me yet. Grab a bunch of friends and have a fiesta, raw vegan style. If you're short on time, you can use lettuce leaves instead of making the soft taco shells.

Soft taco shells

200 g (7 oz/1 cup) corn kernels
350 g (12 oz/2 cups) peeled and chopped zucchini (courgette)
55 g (2 oz/½ cup) linseed (flaxseed) meal
3 tablespoons roughly chopped coriander (cilantro)

Mushroom taco mince

90 g (3¼ oz/1 cup) sliced shiitake mushrooms
150 g (5½ oz/2 cups) sliced Swiss brown mushrooms
75 g (2½ oz/1 cup) sliced oyster mushrooms
225 g (8 oz/1½ cups) sun-dried tomatoes, soaked in filtered alkaline water for 1 hour, drained
1½ tablespoons ground cumin
2 teaspoons ground coriander
3 tablespoons chopped coriander (cilantro)
1 teaspoon onion powder
1 teaspoon garlic powder
1 tomato, seeded and chopped
2 garlic cloves, peeled
2 tablespoons cold-pressed extra virgin olive oil

Salsa

600 g (1 lb 5 oz/3 cups) diced tomatoes
175 g (6 oz/1 cup) diced cucumber
1 small red onion, finely chopped
25 g (1 oz/½ cup) finely chopped coriander (cilantro)
1 garlic clove, crushed
juice of 1 lime
Himalayan pink salt or Celtic sea salt, to taste
freshly ground black pepper, to taste

To serve

1 batch Sadhana guacamole (page 122)
1 batch Sour cream (page 78)
1 batch Chimichurri (page 74)
lime wedges

❖ Blend all the taco shell ingredients in a high-speed blender on high speed until smooth.
❖ Line dehydrator trays with non-stick sheets, then spread the taco mixture onto the sheets, into round taco shapes. Dehydrate at 40°C (105°F) for 4 hours, flipping after 2 hours and removing the non-stick sheets. (If you don't have a dehydrator, spread the mixture into rounds on baking trays lined with non-stick sheets and leave in the oven on its lowest setting, with the door slightly ajar, for 1 hour, or until the taco shells are dry to touch, but still pliable.)

❖ Once the taco shells are done, start on the mushroom taco mince. In a food processor, pulse the mushrooms until roughly chopped. Transfer to a mixing bowl and set aside. Add the remaining taco mince ingredients to the food processor and blend on high speed until well combined. Add to the mushrooms and mix together by hand. Set aside.
❖ Toss together all the salsa ingredients.
❖ To serve, plate all the individual components in small bowls and serve tapas style, to enjoy with your crew.

SADHANA LASAGNE

SERVES 4–6

When we first opened Sadhana Kitchen, this was the first raw meal I ever prepared.
It's still our most popular dish, and will probably stay on the menu for years to come.
This recipe was originally much more complicated, so we have to thank Cathy Mackell,
one of Sadhana's amazing alumni, for giving us the same delicious result,
with much less faffin' about. I hope you love it as much as we do.

6 large zucchini (courgettes),
peeled and cut into 3 mm
(⅛ inch) thick slices (I use
a mandoline for this)
180 g (6 oz/4 cups) baby English
spinach leaves
1 batch Basil, kale & pine nut
pesto (page 94), in a
squeeze bottle
herb sprigs, to garnish
baby salad leaves, sprouts
or microgreens, to serve

Bolognaise
400 g (14 oz/4 cups) activated
walnuts
2 tablespoons dried oregano
1 tablespoon dried sage
pinch of cayenne pepper
175 g (6½ oz/1¼ cups) sun-dried
tomatoes, soaked in alkaline
filtered water for 1 hour,
then drained
200 g (7 oz/1 cup) seeded
and diced tomatoes
125 ml (4 fl oz/½ cup) cold-pressed
extra virgin olive oil
1 tablespoon miso paste
3 tablespoons filtered
alkaline water

Cashew cheeze
620 g (1 lb 6 oz/4 cups)
cashew nuts
1 tablespoon miso paste
125 ml (4 fl oz/½ cup) lemon juice
2 garlic cloves, peeled
4 tablespoons nutritional yeast
2 teaspoons dried thyme
½ teaspoon Himalayan pink salt
or Celtic sea salt

❖ To make the bolognaise, place the walnuts, oregano,
sage and cayenne pepper in a food processor fitted
with an 'S' blade, then pulse until the mixture has the
texture of fine crumbs. Transfer to a mixing bowl.
Now pop the sun-dried tomatoes, fresh tomatoes,
olive oil, miso paste and water in a high-speed
blender and blend until smooth. Add to the crumbled
walnut mixture and use clean hands to mix it all
together until well combined. Set aside.
❖ Clean out the blender, then whiz all the cashew
cheeze ingredients until super smooth. Set aside.
❖ To assemble the lasagne, grab yourself a baking
dish, measuring about 34 x 24 cm (13½ x 9½ inches)
and about 7 cm (2¾ inches) deep.

❖ Layer the components in the following order:
half the zucchini slices (these are your 'pasta sheets'),
a third of the spinach, all the bolognaise, another
third of the spinach, the remaining zucchini slices,
then the remaining spinach. Top the whole thing
with the cashew cheeze.
❖ Set in the fridge for 2 hours.
❖ Remove the lasagne from the fridge. Cut into
portions, and allow to come to room temperature.
❖ To serve, squeeze the pesto over the top of
the lasagne in a pretty pattern. Cut the lasagne
into individual portions and transfer to plates.
Garnish with herb sprigs and serve with a simple
side of baby salad leaves.

REUBEN BAGELS

SERVES 4

This bagel is like a party in your mouth, where the guest list is full of sexy enzyme-rich, nutrient-dense foods, and unhealthy crap isn't invited. This is my raw vegan take on the traditional heart attack–inducing Reuben bagel.

4 Bagels (page 60)

Filling
225 g (8 oz/1 cup) Brazil nut cheddar cream cheeze
   (page 79)
250 g (9 oz/1 cup) Eggplant pastrami (page 128)
150 g (5½ oz/1 cup) Sauerkraut (page 84)
60 g (2¼ oz/1 cup) alfalfa sprouts

✤ Cut each bagel in half. Take the bottom piece of each bagel and spread it with a generous amount of Brazil nut cream cheeze. Top with some eggplant pastrami, sauerkraut and alfalfa sprouts.
✤ Take the top piece of the bagels and slather the inside face with some more Brazil nut cream cheeze. Place on the bottom bagel pieces and serve.

BLAT SANDWICH ON ONION BREAD

SERVES 4

When I made this for the first time, I was pretty stoked. So stoked, in fact, that I entered into a committed and exclusive relationship with it every single lunchtime for the next 4 weeks.

8 pieces of Onion flat bread (page 59)
1 batch Kumara chips (page 136)

Filling
1 batch Basil aioli (page 124)
8 baby cos (romaine) lettuce leaves
2 large tomatoes, sliced
2 large avocados, flesh sliced into wedges about
   1 cm (½ inch) thick
250 g (9 oz/1 cup) Coconut bacon (page 128)

✤ Spread four pieces of onion flat bread with a generous amount of basil aioli.
✤ Top each with one lettuce leaf, two tomato slices, the avocado wedges, coconut bacon, then another lettuce leaf.
✤ Slather the remaining flat breads with more basil aioli, then pop the lids on the sandwiches.
✤ Serve with a side of kumara chips.

EGGPLANT INVOLTINI
WITH SQUASH MASH

SERVES 4

Want to wine and dine someone sexy? Try this recipe out. Pair it with
a bottle of good vegan red wine and it's on like Donkey Kong.

Involtini sauce

115 g (4 oz/2 cups) dehydrated
tomato slices (see Tip)
55 g (2 oz/1 cup) dehydrated red
capsicum (pepper) slices
(see Tip)
50 g (1¾ oz/⅓ cup) sun-dried
tomatoes, soaked in filtered
alkaline water for 1 hour,
then drained (see Tip)
1 tablespoon balsamic vinegar
1 tablespoon coconut sugar
2 garlic cloves, peeled
3 tablespoons cold-pressed extra
virgin olive oil

Involtini mince

240 g (8½ oz/1½ cups) activated
almonds, milled to fine crumbs
in a food processor

2 small carrots, peeled and roughly
chopped, then finely chopped
in a food processor
100 g (3½ oz/1 cup) finely
diced mushrooms
80 g (2¾ oz/½ cup) finely diced
red capsicum (pepper)
100 g (3½ oz/¾ cup) finely
diced celery
250 g (9 oz/1½ cups) finely diced
zucchini (courgette)
110 g (3¾ oz/¾ cup) sun-dried
tomatoes, soaked in filtered
alkaline water for 1 hour,
then drained
2 large medjool dates, pitted
1 garlic clove, peeled
½ teaspoon ground cloves
2 teaspoons ground cinnamon
2 teaspoons apple cider vinegar

250 ml (9 fl oz/1 cup) filtered
alkaline water

Squash mash

350 g (12 oz/2 cups) roughly
chopped yellow (baby pattypan)
squash
155 g (5½ oz/1 cup) activated
cashew nuts
1½ tablespoons nutritional yeast
2 teaspoons miso paste
1 tablespoon lemon juice
½ teaspoon Himalayan pink salt
or Celtic sea salt

To serve

1 batch Eggplant pastrami
(page 128)
curly parsley sprigs, to garnish

❖ Blend all the involtini sauce ingredients in a high-
speed blender until smooth. Transfer to a squeeze
bottle and set aside.

❖ To make the involtini mince, place the almonds in a
food processor and chop until milled into fine crumbs.
Tip into a mixing bowl. Very finely chop the carrot in
the food processor, then add to the almonds, along
with the mushroom, capsicum, celery and zucchini.

❖ Now blend the sun-dried tomatoes, dates, garlic,
cloves, cinnamon, vinegar and water in the blender on
high speed until smooth. Add to the almond mixture
and combine well, using your hands. Set aside.

❖ Clean out the food processor and fit it with an 'S'
blade. Whiz the squash mash ingredients until 'fluffy'.

❖ To assemble the dish, place a scoop of squash mash
on four plates. Take three pieces of eggplant pastrami
for each plate, and fill each with 1 tablespoon of the
involtini mince. Roll to contain the mince and place
on the mash, seam side down. Squeeze the involtini
sauce over the top. Garnish with parsley and serve.

 TIP To dehydrate tomato and capsicum slices,
spread them on non-stick dehydrator trays
and dehydrate at 40°C (105°F) for 4 hours.
(If you don't have a dehydrator, leave them
in the oven on its lowest setting, with the
door slightly ajar, for 40 minutes.)
While soaking the sun-dried tomatoes, soak an
extra quantity for the Involtini mince mixture.

MUSHROOM, SPINACH & CARAMELISED ONION QUICHE

SERVES 4–6

This is another old-school Sadhana Kitchen dish, which featured on the menu when we first opened. It now lives on in mini form as part of our organic, raw vegan high tea. It goes down a treat with a side salad of baby greens.

Marinated filling
180 g (6 oz/2 cups) sliced button mushrooms
90 g (3¼ oz/2 cups) baby English spinach leaves, shredded
½ teaspoon Himalayan pink salt or Celtic sea salt
1 tablespoon lemon juice

Quiche base
390 g (13¾ oz/2½ cups) activated cashew nuts
4 tablespoons linseed (flaxseed) meal
1 garlic clove, peeled
1 tablespoon nutritional yeast
1 tablespoon cold-pressed extra virgin olive oil
½ teaspoon Himalayan pink salt or Celtic sea salt
125 ml (4 fl oz/½ cup) filtered alkaline water
1 tablespoon lemon juice

Zucchini & cashew filling
350 g (12 oz/2 cups) chopped zucchini (courgette)
125 ml (4 fl oz/½ cup) filtered alkaline water
235 g (8½ oz/1½ cups) activated cashew nuts
3 tablespoons miso paste
2 teaspoons lemon juice
½ onion, roughly chopped
3 tablespoons nutritional yeast
½ teaspoon Himalayan pink salt or Celtic sea salt

To serve
1 batch Caramelised onion (page 96)
curly parsley, to garnish

❖ Combine the marinated filling ingredients in a bowl and massage well. Leave to sit at room temperature while preparing the rest of the recipe.
❖ Place all the quiche base ingredients in a food processor. Blend until a chunky dough forms, then press into a 23 cm (9 inch) tart (flan) tin. Set aside.
❖ Put the zucchini & cashew filling ingredients in a high-speed blender, placing the zucchini in the bottom of the jug for easy blending. Blend until smooth.

❖ Fold the marinated filling ingredients into the mixture, then pour into the tart tin.
❖ Dehydrate at 40°C (105°F) for 24 hours, or until set. (If you don't have a dehydrator, leave the tart in the oven on its lowest setting, with the door slightly ajar, for 2 hours.)
❖ Top with caramelised onion, garnish with parsley and cut into eight pieces to serve.

HAWAIIAN & SMOKY BBQ PIZZAS

EACH VERSION SERVES
6–8 PARTY PEOPLE

Pizza is one of those all-time party favourites. These raw vegan versions are zinging with flavour, so make loads of them to share — I promise you, if your peeps like pizza, they're gonna love this one!

Hawaiian

6–8 small Pizza bases (page 58)

1 batch Tomato sauce (page 114)

320 g (11¼ oz/2 cups) diced pineapple

500 g (1 lb 2 oz/2 cups) Coconut bacon (page 128), sliced into 1 cm (½ inch) strips

155 g (5½ oz/1 cup) diced red capsicum (pepper)

1 large red onion, sliced into super-thin rings (I use a mandoline for this)

90 g (3¼ oz/2 cups) baby English spinach leaves, finely shredded

1 batch Aged macadamia cheeze (page 79), blended with 50 ml (1¾ fl oz) water, then transferred to a squeeze bottle

Smoky BBQ

6–8 small Pizza bases (page 58)

1 batch Smoky BBQ sauce (page 114)

500 g (1 lb 2 oz/2 cups) Coconut bacon (page 128), sliced into 1 cm (½ inch) strips

1 handful Eggplant pastrami (page 128)

155 g (5½ oz/1 cup) diced red capsicum (pepper)

90 g (3¼ oz/2 cups) baby English spinach leaves, finely shredded

155 g (5½ oz/1 cup) pine nuts

1 batch Caramelised onion (page 96)

1 handful Smoky BBQ kale chips (page 132)

1 batch Aged macadamia cheeze (page 79), blended with 50 ml (1¾ fl oz) water, then transferred to a squeeze bottle

❖ Place a pizza base on a clean, flat surface. Spread a generous amount of tomato sauce or smoky barbecue sauce over it.

❖ Sprinkle your chosen toppings over the pizza base. Finish by squeezing some macadamia cheeze all over that tasty, tasty thing. Repeat to make more pizzas.

❖ Cut into slices to serve.

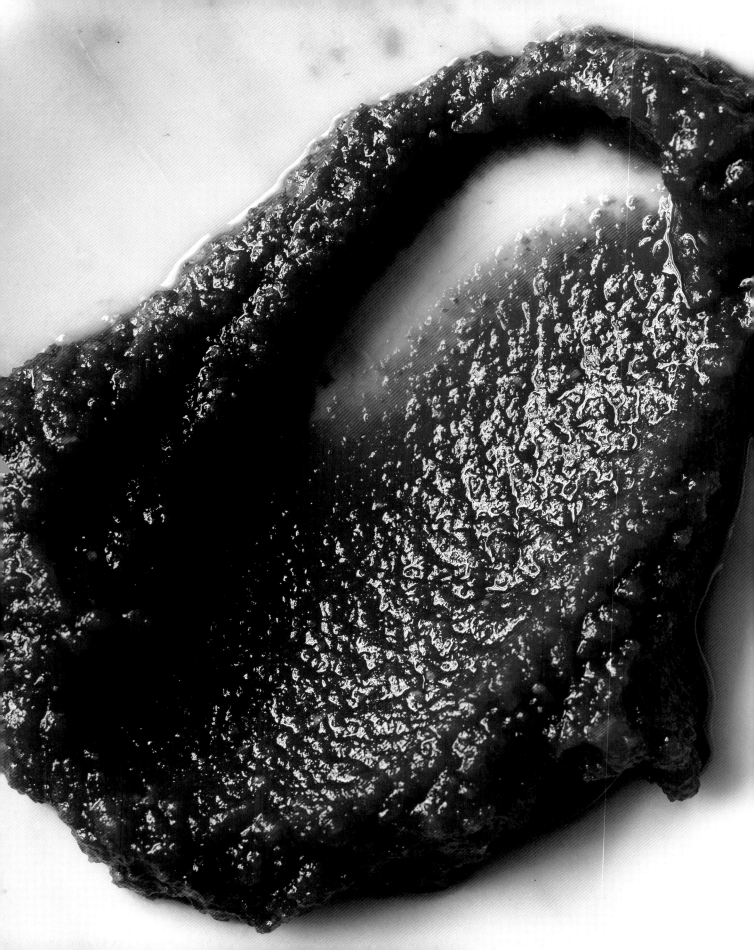

SAVOURY CONDIMENTS

SAVOUR THE FLAVOURS

These fabulous dressings, dips and sauces will take
any main meal to the next level. Keep them on hand
for quick throw-together meals on the go.

TOMATO SAUCE

MAKES 250 ML
(9 FL OZ/1 CUP)

Tomato sauce goes with lots of things, and this raw vegan version is much better for you than some of the brands available in stores, which are highly processed and contain nasties like high-fructose corn syrup. Serve it on the side of some of your cooked meals, or use it with some of the raw recipes in this book.

75 g (2½ oz/½ cup) sun-dried tomatoes
100 g (3½ oz/½ cup) seeded and chopped fresh tomato
1½ tablespoons apple cider vinegar
¼ teaspoon garlic powder
¼ teaspoon onion powder
3 tablespoons coconut nectar
¼ teaspoon Himalayan pink salt or Celtic sea salt

❖ Soak the sun-dried tomatoes in some filtered alkaline water for 1 hour.
❖ Place the sun-dried tomatoes, along with 1½ tablespoons of their soaking water, in a high-speed blender. Add the remaining ingredients and blend on high speed until super smooth.
❖ The sauce will keep in a clean airtight jar in the fridge for 5 days.

SMOKY BBQ SAUCE

MAKES 250 ML
(9 FL OZ/1 CUP)

Like tomato sauce, this guy can be enjoyed with traditional foods, as a healthier alternative. It's also pretty amazing when used as pizza sauce, and as a delicious coating for kale chips (page 132).

150 g (5½ oz/1 cup) sun-dried tomatoes
90 g (3¼ oz/½ cup) pitted medjool dates
1 teaspoon ground cumin
1 teaspoon smoked paprika
¼ teaspoon cayenne pepper
1 garlic clove, peeled
2 tablespoons cold-pressed extra virgin olive oil
2 tablespoons apple cider vinegar
3 tablespoons tamari
125 ml (4 fl oz/½ cup) filtered alkaline water

❖ Soak the sun-dried tomatoes in some filtered alkaline water for 1 hour.
❖ Drain the sun-dried tomatoes and place in a high-speed blender. Add all the remaining ingredients and blend until smooth.
❖ The sauce will keep in a clean airtight jar in the fridge for 5 days.

SWEET CHILLI SAUCE

MAKES 250 ML
(9 FL OZ/1 CUP)

Sweet chilli sauce is an awesome base for dressings, and makes a nice dipping sauce served alongside pretty much anything. This is especially great in a raw vegan Banh mi (page 98).

40 g (1½ oz/¼ cup) sun-dried tomatoes
80 g (2¾ oz/½ cup) chopped red capsicum (pepper)
4 tablespoons apple cider vinegar
3 tablespoons lime juice
1 garlic clove, peeled
3 tablespoons coconut nectar
¼ teaspoon Himalayan pink salt or Celtic sea salt
¼ red onion, finely diced
2 large hot red chillies, seeded and finely chopped
1 tablespoon grated fresh ginger

❖ Soak the sun-dried tomatoes in some filtered alkaline water for 1 hour.
❖ Drain the sun-dried tomatoes and place in a high-speed blender. Add all the ingredients except the onion, chilli and ginger, then blend on high speed until super smooth.
❖ Pour into a clean glass jar and stir in the remaining ingredients. Seal the jar and store in the fridge. The sauce will keep for 5 days.

SADHANA HOT SAUCE

MAKES 250 ML
(9 FL OZ/1 CUP)

Quite possibly one of the best condiments ever made, this is my raw and vegan take on a sriracha sauce. Add it to anything you'd like to have a bit of a kick.

80 g (2¾ oz/½ cup) chopped red capsicum (pepper)
65 g (2¼ oz/½ cup) fresh green jalapeño chillies, stems removed
4 long red chillies, stems and seeds removed
125 ml (4 fl oz/½ cup) apple cider vinegar
4 garlic cloves, peeled
4 tablespoons coconut nectar
1 tablespoon Himalayan pink salt or Celtic sea salt

❖ Place all the ingredients in a food processor. Pulse until well combined, but still chunky.
❖ Pour into a glass jar and cover the opening with muslin (cheesecloth) or a tea towel (dish towel). Secure the fabric in place with a rubber band. Leave to ferment, away from direct sunlight, but in a warm place, for 24–48 hours.
❖ Once fermented, transfer to a high-speed blender and blend until smooth. Pour into a clean, airtight glass jar and seal the lid.
❖ The sauce will keep in the fridge for 5 days.

HOLLANDAISE SAUCE

MAKES 250 ML
(9 FL OZ/1 CUP)

This stuff is like unicorn tears — it's magical, delicious, and almost too good to be true. It's the bees knees on our Mushrooms benedict (page 42), but is also great as a salad dressing, and in wraps and sandwiches too.

155 g (5½ oz/1 cup) activated cashew nuts
juice of 1 lemon
½ teaspoon black salt
1 tablespoon nutritional yeast
2 heaped teaspoons French mustard
½ teaspoon ground turmeric
170 ml (5½ fl oz/⅔ cup) filtered alkaline water

❖ Blend all the ingredients in a high-speed blender until smooth.
❖ The sauce will keep in a clean glass jar in the fridge for 5 days.

GARLIC SAUCE

MAKES 250 ML
(9 FL OZ/1 CUP)

In the suburb where I grew up, there's a charcoal chicken shop that has the most ridiculous (in a good way) garlic sauce. Like it's *so so so so good* I would literally mix it up with rice and just eat that for dinner and be completely happy. Unfortunately, that doesn't do much for variety, excitement or meeting my daily nutritional requirements.

This raw vegan version keeps it nice and healthy, and you can add it to anything for a hit of flavour — and very distinctive breath! It's so worth it though.

235 g (8½ oz/1½ cups) activated cashew nuts
4 tablespoons apple cider vinegar
4 tablespoons lemon juice
4 tablespoons coconut nectar
32 garlic cloves, peeled
250 ml (9 fl oz/1 cup) filtered alkaline water
1 teaspoon Himalayan pink salt or Celtic sea salt

❖ Blend all the ingredients in a high-speed blender until smooth. Pour into a clean, airtight glass jar and seal the lid.
❖ The sauce will keep in the fridge for 5 days.

KECAP MANIS

**MAKES 250 ML
(9 FL OZ/1 CUP)**

Kecap manis is a sweet soy sauce that is used a lot in Indonesian cooking. It's also a great addition to Asian-inspired dishes.

125 ml (4 fl oz/½ cup) tamari
125 ml (4 fl oz/½ cup) coconut nectar
1 teaspoon grated fresh ginger
1 star anise

❖ Blend all the ingredients in a high-speed blender until smooth. (If you don't have a high-speed blender, it's best to grind the star anise to a powder using a spice grinder, before adding it to your blender.)
❖ Pour into a clean, airtight glass jar and seal the lid.
❖ The sauce will keep in the fridge for 5 days.

SWEET MUSTARD DRESSING

**MAKES 250 ML
(9 FL OZ/1 CUP)**

Even the fussiest salad-leaf haters will love their greens when drizzled with this deliciously luscious dressing. A little goes a long way in terms of flavour.

2 heaped tablespoons dijon mustard
185 ml (6 fl oz/¾ cup) cold-pressed extra virgin olive oil
3 tablespoons coconut nectar
½ teaspoon Himalayan pink salt or Celtic sea salt

❖ Blend all the ingredients in a high-speed blender until smooth. Transfer to a clean squeeze bottle and seal the lid.
❖ The dressing will keep in the fridge for 5 days.

GINGER & MISO DRESSING

MAKES 250 ML
(9 FL OZ/1 CUP)

This dressing goes amazingly well with seaweed dishes. Grab a bunch of your favourite vegies, add some kelp noodles, sliced nori sheets and wakame, add a drizzle of this, and you have yourself a super-tasty salad.

250 ml (9 fl oz/1 cup) filtered alkaline water
3 tablespoons cold-pressed extra virgin olive oil
3 tablespoons tahini
3 tablespoons coconut nectar
2 tablespoons red or white miso paste
1 tablespoon apple cider vinegar
2 teaspoons lime juice
5 cm (2 inch) knob of fresh ginger, peeled and chopped

❖ Blend all the ingredients in a high-speed blender until smooth. Pour into a clean, airtight glass jar and seal the lid.
❖ The dressing will keep in the fridge for 5 days.

HERBED TAHINI DRESSING

MAKES 250 ML
(9 FL OZ/1 CUP)

Add this nut-free dressing to any meal for an extra flavour hit — it's a daily staple in my household. Also try it as a dip for raw crackers and vegies when you're after a deliciously healthy snack.

3 tablespoons roughly chopped flat-leaf (Italian) parsley
3 tablespoons roughly chopped basil
1 garlic clove, peeled
juice of 1 lemon
3 tablespoons cold-pressed extra virgin olive oil
3 tablespoons tahini
3 tablespoons filtered alkaline water
2 tablespoons coconut nectar
½ teaspoon Himalayan pink salt or Celtic sea salt

❖ Blend all the ingredients in a high-speed blender until smooth. Pour into a clean, airtight glass jar and seal the lid.
❖ The dressing will keep in the fridge for 5 days.

BEET & ORANGE DRESSING

MAKES 250 ML
(9 FL OZ/1 CUP)

If you want to make anything you're eating instantly prettier, add this pink dressing to it. The fact that it's really delicious too is a happy bonus.

115 g (4 oz/¾ cup) peeled and chopped raw beetroot (beet)
250 ml (9 fl oz/1 cup) cold-pressed orange juice
1 garlic clove, peeled
2 tablespoons lemon juice
1 tablespoon lemon zest
1 teaspoon tamari
1 tablespoon coconut nectar
75 g (2½ oz/½ cup) activated sunflower seeds
½ teaspoon Himalayan pink salt or Celtic sea salt

❖ Blend all the ingredients in a high-speed blender until smooth. Pour into a clean, airtight glass jar and seal the lid.
❖ The dressing will keep in the fridge for 3 days.

SRIRACHA MAYO

MAKES 250 G
(9 OZ/1 CUP)

A lovely zingy salad dressing, and another great dipping sauce for sweet potato chips.

3 tablespoons Sadhana hot sauce (page 115)
235 g (8½ oz/1½ cups) activated cashew nuts
185 ml (6 fl oz/¾ cup) filtered alkaline water
4 tablespoons apple cider vinegar
4 tablespoons lemon juice
4 tablespoons cold-pressed extra virgin olive oil
1 tablespoon coconut nectar
2 garlic cloves, peeled
1 teaspoon Himalayan pink salt or Celtic sea salt

❖ Blend all the ingredients in a high-speed blender until smooth. Pour into a clean, airtight glass jar and seal the lid.
❖ The mayo will keep in the fridge for 5 days.

SADHANA GUACAMOLE

MAKES 250 G
(9 OZ/1 CUP)

Who doesn't love a good guacamole? It's such a versatile, tasty thing to have on hand. Enjoy it as a snack with some Zucchini crackers (page 63) and sprouts, or add it to your salads for another flavour burst.

600 g (1 lb 5 oz/4 cups) chopped avocado flesh; you'll need about 3 large avocados
3 garlic cloves, peeled and crushed
juice of 1½ limes
2 tablespoons finely chopped coriander (cilantro)
45 g (1½ oz/⅓ cup) finely chopped red onion
½–1 teaspoon Himalayan pink salt or Celtic sea salt
cold-pressed extra virgin olive oil, for covering the guacamole in the fridge

❖ Gently mash the avocado flesh in a bowl, leaving it a bit chunky. Add the garlic, lime juice, coriander, onion and salt to taste, then stir until well combined.
❖ Transfer to a clean glass jar. Pour a thin layer of olive oil over the top, to seal the surface.
❖ The guacamole will keep in the fridge for 3 days.

BEETROOT DIP

MAKES 250 G
(9 OZ/1 CUP)

A pretty addition to a meze plate, and delicious dolloped over salads and wraps. I'm known as the person who always packs her own food, and I love taking a jar of this dip to the movies and nomming away happily with some Kumara chips (page 136) and carrot sticks.

150 g (5½ oz/1 cup) peeled and chopped raw beetroot (beet)
80 g (2¾ oz/½ cup) activated cashew nuts
¼ red onion, finely chopped
1 tomato, chopped
1 garlic clove, peeled
3 tablespoons activated sunflower seeds
125 ml (4 fl oz/½ cup) lemon juice
1 tablespoon apple cider vinegar
1 teaspoon mustard
1 teaspoon ground cumin
2 heaped teaspoons carob powder
¼ teaspoon freshly ground black pepper
½ teaspoon Himalayan pink salt or Celtic sea salt

❖ Blend all the ingredients in a high-speed blender until smooth. Pour into a clean, airtight glass jar and seal the lid.
❖ The dip will keep in the fridge for 3 days.

1 SADHANA GUACAMOLE

2 BEETROOT DIP

BASIL AIOLI

**MAKES 250 G
(9 OZ/1 CUP)**

Great as a salad dressing, and perfect as a dipping sauce for Kumara chips (page 136).

235 g (8½ oz/1½ cups) activated cashew nuts
250 ml (9 fl oz/1 cup) filtered alkaline water
4 tablespoons finely chopped basil
4 tablespoons apple cider vinegar
4 tablespoons lemon juice
4 tablespoons cold-pressed extra virgin olive oil
1 tablespoon coconut nectar
2 garlic cloves, peeled
1 teaspoon Himalayan pink salt or Celtic sea salt

❖ Blend all the ingredients in a high-speed blender until smooth.
❖ The aioli will keep in a clean airtight jar in the fridge for 5 days.

TARTARE SAUCE

**MAKES 250 ML
(9 FL OZ/1 CUP)**

This tartare sauce tastes like the real thing. It's awesome — especially with the Mushroom calamari (page 138).

155 g (5½ oz/1 cup) activated cashew nuts, soaked in filtered alkaline water for 1 hour, then drained
125 ml (4 fl oz/½ cup) filtered alkaline water
1 tablespoon apple cider vinegar
2 teaspoons lemon juice
½ teaspoon garlic powder
½ teaspoon Himalayan pink salt or Celtic sea salt
90 g (3¼ oz/½ cup) dill pickles, finely chopped, plus 1 tablespoon of the pickle brine
4 tablespoons finely chopped spring onion (scallion)
2 tablespoons chopped dill

❖ Blend all the ingredients, except the pickles, spring onion and dill, in a high-speed blender until smooth.
❖ Pour into a clean glass jar and stir in the remaining ingredients. Seal the jar and store in the fridge.
❖ The sauce will keep in the fridge for 5 days.

TOMATO, PAPRIKA & ZUCCHINI HUMMUS

MAKES 250 G
(9 OZ/1 CUP)

For a quick and easy snack, this hummus is the bomb. Try it with vegie sticks and Sadhana guacamole (page 122), or piled onto your favourite salads and wraps. Definitely a good one to have in the fridge to liven up any meal.

150 g (5½ oz/1 cup) sun-dried tomatoes
350 g (12 oz/2 cups) peeled and diced zucchini (courgette)
1 teaspoon smoked paprika
135 g (4¾ oz/½ cup) tahini
125 ml (4 fl oz/½ cup) lemon juice
3 garlic cloves, peeled
2 teaspoons ground cumin
2 tablespoons nutritional yeast
3 tablespoons cold-pressed extra virgin olive oil, plus extra oil for covering the hummus in the fridge
½–1 teaspoon Himalayan pink salt or Celtic sea salt
filtered alkaline water, as needed

❖ Soak the sun-dried tomatoes in some filtered alkaline water for 1 hour.
❖ Drain the sun-dried tomatoes and place in a high-speed blender. Add all the remaining ingredients and blend until smooth, adding some water in small amounts as needed.
❖ Transfer to a clean glass jar. Pour a thin layer of extra olive oil over the top, to seal the surface.
❖ The hummus will keep in the fridge for 3 days.

CHILLI JAM

MAKES 250 G
(9 OZ/1 CUP)

A really hot guy once made me chilli jam, but forgot to mention it had fish sauce in it. Fail! Spicy, nutritious and flavoursome, this raw vegan version is seriously addictive. That hot guy is now my boyfriend, so I think that speaks for itself.

25 g (1 oz/½ cup) roughly chopped coriander (cilantro)
2 garlic cloves, peeled
3 tablespoons roughly chopped lemongrass, pale part only
4 long red chillies, seeded
2.5 cm (1 inch) knob of fresh ginger, peeled and roughly chopped
125 ml (4 fl oz/½ cup) coconut nectar
1 teaspoon dulse flakes
2 tablespoons tamari
2 tablespoons chia seeds

❖ Blend all the ingredients, except the chia seeds, in a high-speed blender until smooth.
❖ Pour into a bowl and whisk in the chia seeds until the mixture thickens to the consistency of jam.
❖ Pour into a clean, airtight glass jar and seal the lid.
❖ The jam will keep in the fridge for 5 days.

SNACKS & SIDES

NOT JUST CARROT STICKS & DIP

Someone once asked me, what good is eating really
healthy meals if you end up snacking on crap anyway?
Good point! These snacks and sides are moreish,
satisfying and really, really tasty. They're also packed
full of easily digestible nutrients.

COCONUT BACON

SERVES 4 HUNGRY SNACKERS, OR 8 NIBBLERS

I'm so stoked this recipe exists — but almost wish it didn't, because I want to eat it all the time. As a kid, I used to love the heck out of bacon, and when I grew up and got a job, two bacon and egg rolls with barbecue sauce were my jam. These days, I stick to this coconut bacon to get an amazing flavour hit. It goes well with pretty much anything.

Make heaps, because if you're anything like me, you'll be munching on these on the regular.

325 g (11½ oz/4 cups) young coconut, flesh sliced into
   bite-sized pieces
125 ml (4 fl oz/½ cup) tamari
3 tablespoons coconut nectar
2 tablespoons smoked paprika
1 tablespoon garlic powder
1 tablespoon onion powder
1 tablespoon cold-pressed sesame oil

❖ Pop all the ingredients in a large mixing bowl, mix together well, then leave to marinate for 20 minutes.
❖ Place on dehydrator trays lined with non-stick sheets and dehydrate at 40°C (105°F) for 12 hours. Flip the coconut pieces over and dehydrate for a further 4 hours; I like them crispy on the outside but still juicy in the middle. (If you don't have a dehydrator, place the coconut pieces on baking trays lined with non-stick sheets and leave in the oven on its lowest setting, with the door slightly ajar, for 1 hour.)
❖ Store in an airtight container in the fridge for up to 3 days; warm in the dehydrator or oven before serving.

EGGPLANT PASTRAMI

SERVES 4 HUNGRY SNACKERS, OR 8 NIBBLERS

Like Coconut bacon (see left), this dish goes well with just about anything. Pop some in a wrap, on top of salads, or on the side of your meals. It's also great in sandwiches.

2 large eggplants (aubergines), cut into 5 mm (¼ inch)
   thin rounds
125 ml (4 fl oz/½ cup) tamari
4 tablespoons coconut nectar
4 tablespoons cold-pressed extra virgin olive oil
3 tablespoons nutritional yeast
2 tablespoons ground sumac
1 tablespoon smoked paprika
2 tablespoons dried oregano
1 tablespoon cold-pressed sesame oil
1 teaspoon Himalayan pink salt or Celtic sea salt
1 teaspoon freshly ground black pepper

❖ Pop all the ingredients in a large mixing bowl, mix together well, then leave to marinate for 20 minutes.
❖ Place on dehydrator trays lined with non-stick sheets and dehydrate at 40°C (105°F) for 12 hours. Flip the eggplant slices over and dehydrate for a further 4 hours; I like them crispy on the outside but still juicy in the middle. (If you don't have a dehydrator, place the eggplant slices on baking trays lined with non-stick sheets and leave in the oven on its lowest setting, with the door slightly ajar, for 1 hour.)
❖ Store in an airtight container in the fridge for up to 3 days; warm in the dehydrator or oven before serving.

SPICY CORN CHIPS

SERVES 4 HUNGRY
SNACKERS, OR 8 NIBBLERS

Serve these spicy little numbers with Guacamole (page 122) and you've got yourself a darn good snack. Needless to say, they are infinitely better for you than the sort you'll find in supermarket aisles.

600 g (1 lb 5 oz/3 cups) corn kernels
1 yellow capsicum (pepper), seeded and chopped
110 g (3¾ oz/1 cup) linseed (flaxseed) meal
50 g (1¾ oz/½ cup) activated walnuts
1 tablespoon ground cumin
2 teaspoons garlic powder
1 teaspoon chilli powder
3 tablespoons lime juice
freshly ground black pepper, to taste

❖ Place all the ingredients in a food processor and blend on high speed until well combined.
❖ Spread the mixture onto dehydrator trays lined with non-stick sheets. Using a butter knife, score the mixture with triangle shapes, for easy cutting later on.
❖ Dehydrate for 12 hours. Flip the corn mixture over and remove the non-stick sheets. Score more triangles into the side that is facing up, then dehydrate for a further 6 hours. (If you don't have a dehydrator, place the mixture on baking trays lined with non-stick sheets and leave in the oven on its lowest setting, with the door slightly ajar, for 1 hour, then flip and dehydrate on the other side for 15 minutes.)
❖ Once set, cut into corn chips, along the scored lines.
❖ Store in an airtight container at room temperature. The corn chips will keep for 7 days.

SUMMER ROLLS

SERVES 4 HUNGRY
SNACKERS, OR 8 NIBBLERS

Rice paper rolls are one of my go-to fresh and easy snacks. Sometimes I eat lots of them for a deliciously light meal! This version uses my Beet it pink wraps instead of rice paper to keep it all raw.

Dipping sauce
2 heaped tablespoons Chilli jam (page 125)
1 heaped tablespoon tahini
juice of 1 lime
1 tablespoon tamari

Filling
1 batch Chilli jam (page 125)
125 g (4½ oz/2 cups) alfalfa sprouts
90 g (3¼ oz/1 cup) julienned carrots
175 g (6 oz/1 cup) cucumber, cut into 5 mm (¼ inch) sticks
155 g (5½ oz/1 cup) red capsicum (pepper), cut into 5 mm (¼ inch) strips
2 large mangoes, flesh cut into 1 cm (½ inch) strips
2 large avocados, flesh cut into 1 cm (½ inch) strips

To serve
8 Beet it wraps (page 62), cut in half

❖ Place the dipping sauce ingredients in a small bowl and whisk thoroughly until well combined. Set aside.
❖ To assemble the rolls, place a wrap on a chopping board and spread with 1 teaspoon of the chilli jam. Now line up one-eighth of the other filling ingredients, right in the middle of the wrap, starting with a line of alfalfa sprouts, and stacking with the same amount of the remaining ingredients. Roll up away from you, sealing the edge of the wrap with some filtered alkaline water.
❖ Now make another seven rolls in the same way.
❖ Serve straightaway, with the dipping sauce.

1 SMOKY BBQ KALE CHIPS

2 MADRAS CURRY
KALE CHIPS

3 EGGPLANT PASTRAMI

4 SPICY CORN CHIPS

5 CHEEZY CHEDDAR
KALE CHIPS

6 COCONUT BACON

Recipes page 128, 129, 132

MADRAS CURRY KALE CHIPS

SERVES 4 HUNGRY SNACKERS, OR 8 NIBBLERS

Packed with vital nutrients, kale chips really satisfy when you need a crunchy, moreish snack. The Madras curry version has a bit of heat; also try the yummy smoky and cheezy variations below.

1 large bunch (550 g/1 lb 4 oz)
   curly kale

Madras curry kale chips
310 g (11 oz/2 cups) activated
   cashew nuts
250 ml (9 fl oz/1 cup) filtered
   alkaline water
2 tablespoons Madras
   curry powder
4 tablespoons nutritional yeast
1 garlic clove, peeled
Himalayan pink salt or Celtic
   sea salt, to taste

Smoky BBQ kale chips
1 batch Smoky BBQ sauce
   (page 114)

Cheezy cheddar kale chips
1 batch Brazil nut cheddar
   cream cheeze (page 79)

❖ Wash the kale well, then discard the stems, keeping the leaves as large as possible, as they shrink a lot in the dehydrator. Drain the kale well, shaking off all the excess moisture, then place in a large mixing bowl.
❖ If making the **Madras curry kale chips,** combine the ingredients in a high-speed blender and blend on high speed until smooth. Add freshly ground black pepper to taste. Pour the curry mixture over the kale and mix by hand, being sure to thoroughly massage the mixture into the kale.
❖ If making the **Smoky BBQ kale chips** or **Cheezy cheddar kale chips,** add the smoky BBQ sauce or Brazil nut cheddar cream cheeze to the kale and mix by hand, thoroughly massaging the mixture into the kale.
❖ Spread the kale on dehydrator trays. Dehydrate for 4–6 hours at 40°C (105°F), until crispy. (If you don't have a dehydrator, spread the kale on baking trays and leave in the oven on its lowest setting, with the door slightly ajar, for 2 hours.)
❖ Store in an airtight container in the fridge for up to 1 week.

MUSHROOM & PICKLED GINGER COCONUT DUMPLINGS

SERVES 4 HUNGRY SNACKERS, OR 8 NIBBLERS

I love dumplings. I like to think of myself as a dumpling connoisseur,
trying vegan dumplings at every place that serves them.
This super-tasty raw vegan version makes a pretty special starter
for a raw dinner party. And the bonus? Introducing people you
love to life-changing, life-giving food.

Filling
180 g (6 oz/2 cups) finely diced
    shiitake mushrooms
40 g (1½ oz/⅓ cup) finely chopped
    spring onion (scallion)
3 tablespoons finely chopped
    coriander (cilantro)
3 tablespoons finely chopped
    Pickled ginger (page 82)
2 tablespoons tamari
1 teaspoon cold-pressed sesame oil

To serve
1 batch Coconut wraps (page 63)
    shaped into 10 cm (4 inch)
    rounds
Sadhana hot sauce (page 115)
tamari, for dipping

❖ Place all the filling ingredients in a mixing bowl and massage together
using your hands until well combined. Cover and leave to marinate for
20 minutes.
❖ To assemble, place a coconut wrap on a chopping board. Place about
1 tablespoon of the filling mixture in the middle of the wrap. Wet the
edge of the wrap with filtered alkaline water and fold in half, pressing
the edges together to seal, to make a dumpling shaped like a half-moon.
❖ Repeat with the remaining wraps and filling.
❖ Serve the dumplings on a platter, with some Sadhana hot sauce and
a little bowl of tamari on the side.
❖ The dumplings can be made days or weeks ahead and frozen in an
airtight container. Simply thaw them at room temperature when needed.

**1 CHEEZY PEA &
CAULIFLOWER CROQUETTES**

2 KUMARA CHIPS

3 SUMMER ROLLS

**4 MUSHROOM & PICKLED
GINGER COCONUT
DUMPLINGS**

Recipes page 129, 133, 136, 137

KUMARA CHIPS

SERVES 4 HUNGRY SNACKERS, OR 8 NIBBLERS

These savoury chips are delicious on their own, as a side to raw sandwiches, or dipped in Sadhana guacamole (page 122). Also try the sweet version below, which is a much healthier version of the Filipino dish, *kamote que,* or deep-fried caramelised sweet potato, which my momma used to make for *merienda* (mid-morning or mid-afternoon snack).

2 large orange sweet potatoes (kumara)

Savoury kumara chips
4 tablespoons cold-pressed extra virgin olive oil
2 tablespoons dill tips
1 teaspoon garlic powder
1 teaspoon onion powder
1 teaspoon Himalayan pink salt or Celtic sea salt

Sweet kumara chips
1 tablespoon cold-pressed extra virgin coconut oil
2 tablespoons dill tips
1 tablespoon ground cinnamon
2 tablespoons coconut nectar
3 tablespoons coconut sugar
½ teaspoon Himalayan pink salt or Celtic sea salt

❖ Peel the sweet potatoes, then cut into thin slices using a mandoline or vegetable peeler. Place in a large mixing bowl.

❖ Add your choice of flavourings, for either the savoury or sweet kumara chips. Toss together, massaging all the ingredients thoroughly into the sweet potato.

❖ Spread the sweet potato slices on dehydrator trays lined with non-stick sheets. Dehydrate for 6 hours on 40°C (105°F), then remove the non-stick sheets and dehydrate another 2 hours, or until crispy. (If you don't have a dehydrator, place the sweet potato slices on baking trays lined with non-stick sheets and leave in the oven on its lowest setting, with the door slightly ajar, for 2 hours.)

❖ Store in an airtight container in the fridge for up to 1 week.

CHEEZY PEA & CAULIFLOWER CROQUETTES

SERVES 4 HUNGRY
SNACKERS, OR 8 NIBBLERS

Got some little babes to feed? Try these out. These crispy little morsels of joy are one of those magical dishes that can even fool kids into thinking they're deep-fried and naughty.

Filling

155 g (5½ oz/1 cup) activated almonds
145 g (5 oz/1 cup) activated sunflower seeds
155 g (5½ oz/1 cup) fresh peas, or thawed frozen peas
60 g (2¼ oz/½ cup) cauliflower florets
80 g (2¾ oz/½ cup) roughly chopped red onion
3 tablespoons lemon juice
3 tablespoons nutritional yeast
3 tablespoons roughly chopped flat-leaf (Italian) parsley
1 teaspoon Himalayan pink salt or Celtic sea salt
125 ml (4 fl oz/½ cup) filtered alkaline water

Breading

80 g (2¾ oz/½ cup) activated cashew nuts
3 tablespoons linseed (flaxseed) meal
1 teaspoon smoked paprika
1 teaspoon freshly ground black pepper
2 tablespoons nutritional yeast
1 teaspoon Himalayan pink salt or Celtic sea salt

To serve

1 batch Basil aioli (page 124)
1 batch Sweet chilli sauce (page 115)

❖ Place all the filling ingredients in a food processor and mix on high speed until well combined.

❖ Toss all the breading ingredients in a bowl, mixing well.

❖ Take 2 heaped tablespoons of the filling mixture at a time and shape into croquettes. Roll the croquettes in the breading and place on mesh dehydrator trays. Dehydrate at 40°C (105°F) for 8 hours, or until the breading is crispy. (If you don't have a dehydrator, place the croquettes on a baking tray and leave in the oven on its lowest setting, with the door slightly ajar, for 1 hour.)

❖ Serve on a platter, with basil aioli and sweet chilli sauce on the side.

MUSHROOM CALAMARI WITH TARTARE SAUCE & PICKLES

SERVES 4 HUNGRY SNACKERS, OR 8 NIBBLERS

People often wonder how much variety you can really have on a high raw, plant-based diet. While I keep most of my meals as simple as possible, I do hanker now and then for comfort food — and what could be more comforting than something deep-fried? Except it's terrible for you, and doesn't make you feel the best afterwards. Fear not, there is a solution. Served warm from the dehydrator, this mushroom dish really seems like it's been deep-fried, but it hasn't, and it's good for you!

Mushroom calamari
10 king oyster mushrooms
   or oyster mushrooms
   (or a mix of both)
2 tablespoons cold-pressed
   extra virgin olive oil
½ teaspoon black salt
1 teaspoon dulse flakes
2 tablespoons lemon juice

Breading
80 g (2¾ oz/¾ cup) golden linseed
   (flaxseed) meal
1 teaspoon garlic granules
1 teaspoon onion granules
2 teaspoons dried parsley flakes
2 teaspoons dried thyme
2 teaspoons chopped rosemary
½ teaspoon black salt
pinch of chilli powder

To serve
Tartare sauce (page 124)
3 tablespoons sliced dill pickles

❖ If using king oyster mushrooms, slice them into circles 1 cm (½ inch) thick. Use an apple corer or small cookie cutter to cut out a hole in the centre. If using oyster mushrooms, slice them into strips.
❖ Pop the mushrooms into a mixing bowl, along with the olive oil, salt, dulse flakes and lemon juice. Mix well, then leave to marinate for 20 minutes.
❖ In a separate bowl, combine all the breading ingredients. Coat the mushrooms with the breading and place on a mesh dehydrator tray. Dehydrate at 40°C (105°F) for 5 hours, or until the outside is crispy.

(If you don't have a dehydrator, place the breaded mushrooms on a baking tray and leave in the oven on its lowest setting, with the door slightly ajar, for 30 minutes.)
❖ Serve with little bowls of the tartare sauce and sliced pickles.
❖ The mushroom calamari keeps in an airtight container in the fridge for 3 days, but is best served warm as it loses its crispness in the fridge; this can be remedied by popping it in the oven or dehydrator for 15 minutes before serving.

SWEET CONDIMENTS

Adding these sweet babes to your favourite desserts
will take them to a whole new level of awesome.
Use them as garnishes, or as a base for your very
own unique creations — the wilder the better.

SALTED CARAMEL SAUCE

MAKES 250 ML
(9 FL OZ/1 CUP)

At Sadhana Kitchen, we pair this delicious sauce with vegan soft serves, and alongside our delicious raw vegan cakes for an extra tasty drizzle. It goes well with anything that needs a boost of smooth, sweet and slightly salty decadence.

250 ml (9 fl oz/1 cup) coconut nectar
1 teaspoon tahini
1 teaspoon maca powder
1 teaspoon mesquite powder
1 teaspoon lucuma powder
½ teaspoon vanilla powder
pinch of Himalayan pink salt or Celtic sea salt

❖ Blend all the ingredients in a high-speed blender until smooth.
❖ Store in a clean, airtight glass jar or squeeze bottle for easy serving. The sauce will keep in the fridge for 5 days.

STRAWBERRY COULIS

MAKES 250 ML
(9 FL OZ/1 CUP)

Pop this wildly coloured coulis into a squeeze bottle to swirl decorative patterns all over your sweet dishes. It's great for drizzling over crepes, or as a garnish for a cheezecake.

75 g (2½ oz/½ cup) strawberries, hulled
125 ml (4 fl oz/½ cup) coconut nectar
½ teaspoon vanilla powder
2 tablespoons lemon juice
2 tablespoons lemon zest
2 tablespoons beetroot (beet) juice (see Tip)

❖ Blend all the ingredients in a high-speed blender until smooth.
❖ Store in a clean, airtight glass jar or squeeze bottle for easy serving. The coulis will keep in the fridge for 3 days.

 TIP To obtain this amount of beetroot juice, pass a 5 cm (2 inch) chunk of beetroot through a cold-press juicer.

MARMALADE

MAKES ABOUT 310 G
(11 OZ/1 CUP)

This raw vegan version of the traditional favourite is delicious served on toasted sprouted bread. You can also add it to a sweet breakfast for an extra burst of flavour, without the guilt.

250 ml (9 fl oz/1 cup) orange juice
3 tablespoons coconut nectar
zest from 1 orange
2 drops of food-grade orange essential oil
2 tablespoons chia seeds

✿ Blend all the ingredients, except the chia seeds, in a high-speed blender until smooth.
✿ Pour into a clean jam jar and stir in the chia seeds. Continue stirring until the chia seeds have absorbed the liquid and have thickened the marmalade.
✿ Seal the jar and store in the fridge. The marmalade will keep for 3 days.

LEMON CURD

MAKES 250 ML
(9 FL OZ/1 CUP)

You can serve this lemon curd on the side of any sweet breakfast — and it's an absolute killer as a filling in Lemon curd tarts (page 156).

235 g (8½ oz/1½ cups) activated cashew nuts
3 tablespoons cold-pressed extra virgin coconut oil
zest and juice of 2 lemons
125 ml (4 fl oz/½ cup) filtered alkaline water
4 tablespoons coconut nectar
pinch of Himalayan pink salt or Celtic sea salt
1 teaspoon psyllium husks

✿ Blend all the ingredients in a high-speed blender until super smooth.
✿ Pour into a clean glass jar. Seal the jar and store in the fridge. The lemon curd will keep for 3 days.

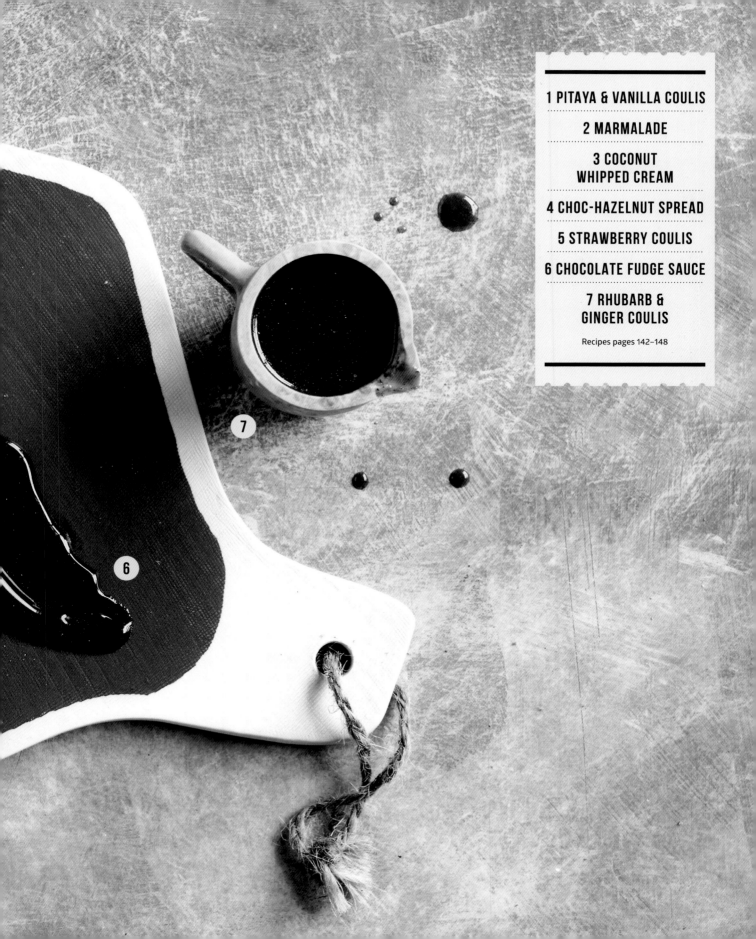

1 PITAYA & VANILLA COULIS

2 MARMALADE

3 COCONUT
WHIPPED CREAM

4 CHOC-HAZELNUT SPREAD

5 STRAWBERRY COULIS

6 CHOCOLATE FUDGE SAUCE

7 RHUBARB &
GINGER COULIS

Recipes pages 142–148

PITAYA & VANILLA COULIS

MAKES 250 ML
(9 FL OZ/1 CUP)

So often, we 'eat with our eyes', which is why pitaya — also known as dragon fruit — is such a wonderful ingredient to have at hand. As well as adding a different flavour dimension to dishes, it has such a vibrant colour that helps dazzle the eye.

Serve some of this coulis with your granola or chia puddings, or alongside cheezecakes, and I promise you'll be sitting down to some of the prettiest food in all the land.

200 g (7 oz/½ cup) peeled and chopped pitaya
125 ml (4 fl oz/½ cup) coconut nectar
2 tablespoons lime juice
2 tablespoons lime zest

❖ Blend all the ingredients in a high-speed blender until smooth.
❖ Store in a clean, airtight glass jar or squeeze bottle for easy serving. The coulis will keep in the fridge for 3 days.

RHUBARB & GINGER COULIS

MAKES 250 ML
(9 FL OZ/1 CUP)

I love serving this coulis on top of raw-food fruit tarts, or drizzled over a huge fruit salad. You could also drizzle some of this into a mason jar and add some cooled green tea and ice for a refreshing iced tea.

60 g (2¼ oz/½ cup) chopped rhubarb (stalk only, no leaves)
2.5 cm (1 inch) knob of fresh ginger, peeled and chopped
125 ml (4 fl oz/½ cup) coconut nectar
½ teaspoon vanilla powder

❖ Blend all the ingredients in a high-speed blender until smooth.
❖ Store in a clean, airtight glass jar or squeeze bottle for easy serving. The coulis will keep in the fridge for 3 days.

CHOC-HAZELNUT SPREAD

MAKES ABOUT 310 G
(11 OZ/1 CUP)

Growing up, I used to keep a large jar of chocolate hazelnut spread beside my bed. I really was a fiend for the stuff. I didn't want to give it up entirely, so I decided to make my own version, free of dairy and refined sugar, to enjoy completely guilt-free.

Rich in healthy monounsaturated and essential fatty acids, this version provides 100% of the recommended daily intake of the potent antioxidant vitamin E in every 15 g (½ oz), and is a good source of minerals such as manganese, potassium, calcium, copper, iron, magnesium, zinc and selenium. It also tastes damn good!

Feed it to yourself, your loved ones, your enemies — just share it with the world, because everybody needs a little choc-hazelnut lovin' once in a while.

115 g (4 oz/1 cup) ground hazelnuts (ground in a high-speed blender)
4 tablespoons raw cacao powder
½ teaspoon vanilla powder
125 ml (4 fl oz/½ cup) coconut nectar
1 tablespoon cold-pressed extra virgin coconut oil, melted
1 tablespoon cacao butter, melted
pinch of Himalayan pink salt or Celtic sea salt

✿ Add all the ingredients to a high-speed blender and blend until smooth, using the tamper to push the mixture onto the blade, because it will be super thick.
✿ Transfer to a clean glass jar, using a spatula. Seal the jar and store in the fridge. The spread will keep for 5 days.

CHOCOLATE FUDGE SAUCE

MAKES 250 ML
(9 FL OZ/1 CUP)

This decadent sauce looks beautiful on a white plate, served alongside your favourite sweets. You can also blend about 4 tablespoons of the sauce with your favourite nut mylk for a delicious chocolatey drink. I also love to drizzle this on fresh berries for a rich yet healthy treat.

250 ml (9 fl oz/1 cup) coconut nectar
4 tablespoons raw cacao powder
1 tablespoon carob powder
½ teaspoon vanilla powder

✿ Blend all the ingredients in a high-speed blender until smooth.
✿ Store in a clean, airtight glass jar or squeeze bottle for easy serving. The sauce will keep in the fridge for 5 days.

147

COCONUT WHIPPED CREAM

MAKES ABOUT 200 G
(7 OZ/1 CUP)

A delectable non-dairy topping for raw vegan scones and pies. Try also serving it alongside fresh fruit, and in place of dairy cream.

80 g (2¾ oz/1 cup) chopped young coconut flesh
125 ml (4 fl oz/½ cup) coconut water
1 teaspoon vanilla powder
stevia, to taste (add very little at a time, as it is very strong)

❖ Blend all the ingredients in a high-speed blender until smooth. Transfer to a clean glass jar. Seal the jar and leave to set in the fridge for 1 hour before serving.
❖ The cream will keep in the fridge for 3 days.

BERRY CHIA JAM

MAKES ABOUT 310 G
(11 OZ/1 CUP)

Here is the ultimate example of something that is usually really sweet and dense in refined sugars being made healthy. You can make this jam using raspberries or blueberries. Add this jam to any sweet breakfast for a dose of colour and deliciousness; the blueberry jam is particularly delicious on fig and date scones.

Raspberry chia jam
250 g (9 oz/2 cups) raspberries
4 tablespoons coconut nectar
4 tablespoons filtered alkaline water
½ teaspoon vanilla powder
2 tablespoons white chia seeds

Blueberry chia jam
310 g (11 oz/2 cups) blueberries
4 tablespoons coconut nectar
4 tablespoons lemon juice
1 tablespoon lemon zest
½ teaspoon vanilla powder
2 tablespoons white chia seeds

❖ Blend all the ingredients, except the chia seeds, in a high-speed blender until smooth.
❖ Pour into a clean, airtight jam jar and stir in the chia seeds. Continue stirring until the chia seeds have absorbed the liquid and expanded into a jam-like consistency.
❖ Seal the jar and store in the fridge. The jam will keep for 3 days.

1 LEMON CURD

2 COCONUT
WHIPPED CREAM

3 RASPBERRY CHIA JAM

4 BLUEBERRY CHIA JAM

Recipes page 143, 148

DESSERTS

Oh sweet, sweet, sexy dessert. The meal that
usually wins over the toughest critics. The one we
turn to in both our darkest and brightest hours.
I've always been very wary of people who don't 'do' dessert
— to me, it's kind of like saying you don't 'do' pleasure. In all
seriousness though, dessert doesn't have to be 'bad' for you.
It can be indulgent and rich and sensual, and just really
damn nice, without the detrimental effects.
The recipes in this chapter are all free of refined sugars and
nasty filler ingredients, yet full of flavour and love. They also
happen to be gluten free, and entirely made from plants.
Creamy stuff without actual cream? Say what?!

CHOC-RASPBERRY CHEEZECAKE

MAKES ONE 23 CM (9 INCH) ROUND CAKE

This is one of the first cakes I made for Sadhana Kitchen. I still remember getting super excited when a yoga teacher and a designer, who are now some of my closest friends, came up to the counter, curious about our raw vegan cakes. I gave Sandy and Alanna a slice of this one to try, and they've been eating our sweet, sweet treats ever since.

Nutty coconut base
155 g (5½ oz/1 cup) activated almonds
150 g (5½ oz/1½ cups) activated walnuts
55 g (2 oz/½ cup) raw cacao powder
180 g (6 oz/2 cups) finely desiccated coconut
360 g (12¾ oz/2 cups) pitted medjool dates
4 tablespoons coconut nectar
1 tablespoon cold-pressed extra virgin coconut oil
pinch of Himalayan pink salt or Celtic sea salt

Choc-raspberry filling
465 g (1 lb/3 cups) activated cashew nuts
3 tablespoons coconut nectar
80 g (2¾ oz/¾ cup) raw cacao powder
375 ml (13 fl oz/1½ cups) filtered alkaline water
1 tablespoon vanilla powder
2.5 cm (1 inch) knob of cacao butter
125 g (4½ oz/1 cup) raspberries
2 tablespoons non-GM soy lecithin

To serve
shaved raw chocolate (optional)
freeze-dried blood orange slices (optional)
125 g (4½ oz/1 cup) raspberries

❖ Process all the nutty coconut base ingredients in a food processor until well combined; the mixture should bind to itself when pressed together between your fingers. Press into a 23 cm (9 inch) round spring-form cake tin.

❖ Put all the filling ingredients in a high-speed blender jug, mixing them with a spatula for easy blending. Blend on high speed until smooth, but for no more than 20 seconds at a time, so you don't burn out the motor.

❖ Pour the filling over the nutty coconut base, then gently tap the cake tin onto a hard surface to get rid of any air bubbles. Set in the fridge overnight, or in the freezer for at least 4 hours.

❖ If serving from the freezer, use a hot knife to ease the cake out of the tin, then let the cake sit at room temperature for 15 minutes.

❖ Just before serving, garnish with shaved chocolate and freeze-dried blood orange slices, if desired, and top with fresh raspberries.

❖ Without the garnishes and raspberries, the cake will keep in an airtight container in the fridge for 5 days, or can be frozen for several months.

STRAWBERRY DOUGHNUTS

MAKES 12

These mini doughnuts are so cute and brilliantly tasty.
You can swap out the strawberries for whatever fruit you like,
and experiment with a bunch of other different flavours.

Doughnuts
180 g (6 oz/1 cup) pitted medjool
    dates, soaked in water for
    1 hour, then drained
25 g (1 oz/1 cup) freeze-dried
    strawberries
115 g (4 oz/¾ cup) activated
    almonds
40 g (1½ oz/¼ cup) activated
    cashew nuts
35 g (1¼ oz/¼ cup) activated
    buckwheat flour
3 tablespoons shredded coconut
3 tablespoons linseed
    (flaxseed) meal
1 tablespoon lucuma powder
pinch of Himalayan pink salt
    or Celtic sea salt
1 tablespoon coconut nectar

Glaze
3 tablespoons cold-pressed
    extra virgin coconut oil
3 tablespoons freeze-dried
    strawberries
1 teaspoon lucuma powder
stevia, to taste (add very little
    at a time, as it is very strong)

To finish
100 g (3½ oz) finely desiccated
    coconut, approximately
3 tablespoons freeze-dried
    strawberries, crushed into
    fine crumbs

❖ Blend all the doughnut ingredients, except the dates and coconut
nectar, in a food processor, to the texture of fine crumbs. Add the
dates and coconut nectar and process until a dough forms. The dough
shouldn't be too sticky, but if it's too dry, add a tiny amount of filtered
alkaline water.

❖ Shape the dough into 12 mini doughnuts and refrigerate for 2–4 hours.

❖ Mix all the glaze ingredients in a high-speed blender until smooth, then
transfer to a bowl. Dip the doughnuts into the glaze, then sprinkle with
the desiccated coconut and freeze-dried strawberry crumbs. Leave to
set in the fridge for a further 1 hour.

❖ The doughnuts will keep in an airtight container in the fridge for
5 days, or can be frozen for several months.

LEMON CURD TARTS

MAKES 24

When you need a sweet fix nice and quick, try these
fabulous little tarts — no baking required, and they don't
even need to set before you can eat them.

Mini tart shells
80 g (2¾ oz/½ cup) activated
    cashew nuts
230 g (8 oz/1½ cups) activated
    macadamia nuts
90 g (3¼ oz/1 cup) finely
    desiccated coconut
180 g (6 oz/1 cup) pitted
    medjool dates
4 tablespoons coconut nectar
2 tablespoons lemon zest

Filling
1 batch Lemon curd (page 143)

Topping
1 batch Coconut whipped cream
    (page 148)
4 tablespoons lemon zest

❖ Process all the tart shell ingredients in a food processor until well
combined. The mixture should bind to itself when pressed together
between your fingers.
❖ Press the mixture into 24 silicone mini tart (flan) moulds, or tart tins
lined with plastic wrap. Turn the tart shells out onto a clean, flat surface.
❖ Spoon the lemon curd into the tart cases. Top with a dollop of coconut
whipped cream, then sprinkle with the lemon zest just before serving.
❖ The tarts will keep in an airtight container in the fridge for 5 days.
Alternatively, the unfilled tart shells can be frozen for several months,
then thawed, filled and topped just before serving.

CHOCOLATE LAVA CAKES WITH STRAWBERRY COULIS CENTRE & WHITE CHOCOLATE FROSTING

MAKES 24

Mi Young, Sadhana's head pastry chef, calls these little lava cakes 'Lover Cakes', because that's what she thought I was calling them when we made them for a Valentine's Day degustation dinner one year. So that's what I call them now, too.

White chocolate frosting
235 g (8½ oz/1½ cups) activated cashew nuts
3 tablespoons cold-pressed extra virgin coconut oil
125 ml (4 fl oz/½ cup) filtered alkaline water
2.5 cm (1 inch) knob of cacao butter
4 tablespoons coconut nectar
2 tablespoons non-GM soy lecithin

Lava cakes
200 g (7 oz/2 cups) activated walnuts
310 g (11 oz/2 cups) activated almonds
185 ml (6 fl oz/¾ cup) coconut nectar
80 g (2¾ oz/¾ cup) raw cacao powder
2 teaspoons vanilla powder

Strawberry coulis centre
1 batch Strawberry coulis (page 142)

To serve
24 fresh raspberries

❖ Blend all the frosting ingredients in a high-speed blender until smooth. Transfer to a container and leave to set in the fridge for 2–4 hours.

❖ Once the frosting has set, start making the lava cakes. Grind the walnuts, then the almonds, to a flour using a high-speed blender, transferring each batch to a food processor. Add the remaining cake ingredients to the food processor and pulse until the mixture has the consistency of a moist cake. The mixture should bind to itself when pressed together between your fingers.

❖ Press some of the cake mixture into 24 mini cupcake tins lined with plastic wrap, or into 24 mini silicone cupcake moulds, keeping some aside for sealing the lava cakes. Use your thumb to press a well into the middle of each one. Spoon in some strawberry coulis.

❖ To seal the cakes, take a 3 cm (1¼ inch) ball of cake mixture and flatten it into a mushroom-like shape using your thumbs. Press on top of a cake, over the coulis, then seal the edges together. Repeat with the remaining cake mixture and lava cakes.

❖ Turn the lava cakes out onto a clean, flat surface. Use a small ice cream scoop to pop a nice round ball of the frosting onto each lava cake. Top each with a single raspberry just before serving.

❖ The cakes will keep in an airtight container in the fridge for 5 days, or can be frozen (without the raspberry on top) for several months.

BANANARAMA CUPCAKES

MAKES 24

Rich in nutrients and utterly delicious, these dainty cupcakes
go really well with the Cheeky chai tonic (page 183) as a
super-charged sweet snack.

155 g (5½ oz/1 cup) activated
   cashew nuts
100 g (3½ oz/1 cup) activated
   walnuts
310 g (11 oz/2 cups) activated
   almonds
125 ml (4 fl oz/½ cup) coconut
   nectar
2 teaspoons vanilla powder
45 g (1½ oz/½ cup) dried bananas,
   chopped
½ banana, mashed
1 tablespoon lemon juice

Macadamia & banana frosting
160 g (5½ oz/1 cup) activated
   macadamia nuts
3 tablespoons cold-pressed extra
   virgin coconut oil
4 tablespoons coconut nectar
1 banana, mashed
1 teaspoon ground cinnamon

Topping
fresh banana slices

✣ Using a high-speed blender, and working in separate batches, grind
the cashews, walnuts and almonds into a flour, tipping each batch into
a mixing bowl.
✣ Add the ground nuts to a food processor. Add the coconut nectar,
vanilla powder, dried banana, mashed banana and lemon juice, then
pulse to the consistency of a moist cake. The mixture should bind to itself
when pressed together between your fingers.
✣ Press the mixture into 24 mini cupcake tins lined with plastic wrap, or
into 24 mini silicone cupcake moulds, then turn the cupcakes out onto a
clean, flat surface.
✣ Blend all the frosting ingredients in a high-speed blender until smooth.
Pop into a piping (icing) bag and pipe onto the cupcakes. Top each
cupcake with a piece of banana just before serving.
✣ The cupcakes will keep in an airtight container in the fridge for 5 days,
or can be frosted and frozen for several months.

CHURROS WITH DARK CHOCOLATE & SALTED CARAMEL SAUCE

SERVES 4

My brother, Mik, loves churros. Growing up we would always make stuff that we liked the sound of. This is a recipe I made up for him to see if he could let the refined sugars go even for just one dish. He definitely could! These smell ridiculously good as they dehydrate, so control yourself and then look forward to devouring it all when it's done.

Churros
185 g (6½ oz/1 cup) activated
    buckwheat groats
155 g (5½ oz/1 cup) activated
    cashew nuts
80 g (2¾ oz/½ cup) activated
    almonds
55 g (2 oz/½ cup) linseed
    (flaxseed) meal
100 g (3½ oz/½ cup) coconut sugar
1½ tablespoons ground cinnamon

1 tablespoon vanilla powder
pinch of Himalayan pink salt or
    Celtic sea salt
125 ml (4 fl oz/½ cup) Coconut mylk
    (page 174)

Dark chocolate
230 g (8 oz/1 cup) cacao butter
55 g (2 oz/½ cup) raw cacao
    powder
50 g (2¾ oz/½ cup) coconut sugar,
    powdered using a coffee grinder
    or high-speed blender

To serve
1 batch Salted caramel sauce
    (page 142)

❖ Place all the churros ingredients, except the coconut mylk, in a food processor and mix to the texture of fine crumbs. Add the coconut mylk and process until a dough forms.

❖ Place the dough in a piping (icing) bag fitted with an open star tip. Pipe 15 cm (6 inch) long churros onto dehydrator trays lined with non-stick sheets. Dehydrate at 40°C (105°F) for 8 hours, then remove the non-stick sheets and dehydrate for a further 2 hours, or until crispy on the outside. (If you don't have a dehydrator, place the churros on baking trays lined with non-stick sheets and leave in the oven on its lowest setting, with the door slightly ajar, for 1½ hours, then flip them over and dehydrate for a further 20 minutes.)

❖ When the churros are ready, prepare the dark chocolate component. Melt the cacao butter in a metal bowl set over a saucepan of gently simmering water, or in a double boiler over low heat. Do not allow to heat over 45°C (115°F); check the temperature using a sugar thermometer. (Alternatively you can

melt the cacao butter in the dehydrator for 1 hour, at 45°C/115°F). Stir until all the lumps are gone, then remove from the heat.

❖ Now stir the cacao powder into the melted cacao butter, making sure there are no powder lumps, BEFORE adding the coconut sugar powder. Whisk vigorously until smooth, or transfer to a high-speed blender and blend on high speed until smooth, taking care not to overheat the mixture.

❖ Transfer the dark chocolate mixture to a large metal bowl and, using a spatula, quickly spread it over the entire surface of the bowl, to lower its temperature. This method of heating and cooling is referred to as 'tempering', and will ensure the chocolate has a glossy shine and will 'snap' nicely when bitten.

❖ Coat about 5 cm (2 inches) of the churros in the dark chocolate, then arrange on a platter with a drizzle of the salted caramel sauce to serve.

❖ The churros will keep in an airtight container in the fridge for 5 days, or can be frozen for several months.

ORANGE & POPPYSEED CAKE

MAKES ONE 23 CM
(9 INCH) ROUND CAKE

Most raw vegan cakes are of the cheesecake variety, but this cake has a texture similar to a baked cake. It reminds me of the awesome orange teacakes I used to buy at my school cafeteria, along with a huge box of hot chips covered in barbecue sauce and gravy. My, how things have changed! Serve this one with herbal tea.

For the cake
450 g (1 lb/5 cups) finely
   desiccated coconut
100 g (3½ oz/1 cup) almond meal
100 g (3½ oz/1 cup) cashew meal
40 g (1½ oz/½ cup) psyllium husks
1 teaspoon vanilla powder
500–625 ml (17–21½ fl oz/2–2½
   cups) cold-pressed orange juice
250 ml (9 fl oz/1 cup) zucchini
   (courgette) purée
3 tablespoons poppy seeds
180 g (6 oz/1 cup) orange zest
125 ml (4 fl oz/½ cup) coconut
   nectar

Cashew & orange icing
155 g (5½ oz/1 cup) activated
   cashew nuts
30 g (1 oz/½ cup) shredded
   coconut
185 ml (6 fl oz/¾ cup) cold-pressed
   extra virgin coconut oil
stevia, to taste (add very little at
   a time, as it is very strong)
250 ml (9 fl oz/1 cup) cold-pressed
   orange juice
2 tablespoons orange zest
1 teaspoon vanilla powder
1 tablespoon non-GM soy lecithin

To garnish
2 tablespoons finely
   desiccated coconut
1 tablespoon orange zest
1 tablespoon poppy seeds

❖ Combine all the cake ingredients in a large non-reactive bowl. Mix together by hand, then knead into a dough. Press the cake mixture into a 23 cm (9 inch) spring-form cake tin lined with baking paper.

❖ Blend all the icing ingredients in a high-speed blender until smooth. Pour over the cake, then decorate with the coconut, orange zest and poppy seeds.

❖ Set in the fridge overnight, or in the freezer for at least 4 hours.

❖ If serving from the freezer, use a hot knife to ease the cake out of the tin, then let the cake sit at room temperature for 15 minutes before cutting.

❖ The cake will keep in an airtight container in the fridge for 5 days, or can be frozen for several months.

APPLE & STRAWBERRY CRUMBLE PIE
WITH RHUBARB & GINGER COULIS

**MAKES ONE 23 CM
(9 INCH) ROUND PIE**

At Sadhana Kitchen, we offer special crumbles such as this during the cooler
months, and serve them with a side of raw vegan coconut soft serve; here,
coconut whipped cream also does the trick. This dish is best served warm,
out of the dehydrator. Enjoy a slice with your favourite herbal tea.

Walnut & date base

40 g (1½ oz/¼ cup) activated
   almonds
100 g (3½ oz/1 cup) activated
   walnuts
45 g (1½ oz/¼ cup) activated
   buckwheat groats
90 g (3¼ oz/1 cup) finely
   desiccated coconut
180 g (6 oz/1 cup) pitted
   medjool dates
4 tablespoons coconut nectar
1 tablespoon lucuma powder
1 teaspoon vanilla powder

Apple purée

2 apples, peeled, cored
   and chopped
1 teaspoon ground cinnamon
2 teaspoons vanilla powder
60 g (2¼ oz/½ cup) sultanas
   (golden raisins)
3 tablespoons coconut syrup
3 tablespoons psyllium husks

Fruit filling

5 apples, peeled and diced
500 g (1 lb 2 oz/3 cups) diced
   strawberries
juice of ½ lemon

To serve

1 batch Coconut whipped cream
   (page 148)
1 batch Rhubarb & ginger coulis
   (page 146), in a squeeze bottle

❖ Process the ingredients for the walnut and date
base in a food processor until well combined. The
mixture should bind to itself when pressed together
between your fingers. Press into a greased 23 cm
(9 inch) pie tin and set aside.

❖ Blend the apple purée ingredients in a high-speed
blender until smooth. Transfer to a large bowl. Add
the fruit filling ingredients and gently mix together
by hand.

❖ Pour the filling over the base and place the whole
tin in the dehydrator. Dehydrate for 4 hours. (If you
don't have a dehydrator, place the pie tin on a baking
tray and leave in the oven on its lowest setting, with
the door slightly ajar, for 30 minutes.)

❖ Serve warm from the dehydrator, with coconut
whipped cream and a drizzle of rhubarb and
ginger coulis.

❖ Without the cream and coulis, the crumble will keep
in an airtight container in the fridge for 5 days, or can
be frozen for several months.

SUPERFOOD CARAMEL SLICE

SERVES 12
SASSY SWEET TOOTHS

This caramel slice is one of our most requested recipes. I remember loving caramel slice before I became vegan, and then loving the super-sugary vegan versions too. After making this one, I had a small piece of that same sugary vegan variety, and realised this caramel slice is actually the best I've ever had. This one will bring all the boys to the yard.

Slice base
80 g (2¾ oz/½ cup) activated almonds
155 g (5½ oz/1 cup) activated cashew nuts
90 g (3¼ oz/½ cup) activated buckwheat groats
180 g (6 oz/2 cups) finely desiccated coconut
360 g (12¾ oz/2 cups) pitted medjool dates
4 tablespoons coconut nectar
1 teaspoon tahini
1 teaspoon maca powder
1 teaspoon lucuma powder
1 teaspoon mesquite powder

Superfood caramel
155 g (5½ oz/1 cup) activated cashew nuts
270 g (9½ oz/1½ cups) pitted medjool dates
125 ml (4 fl oz/½ cup) cold-pressed extra virgin coconut oil
1 teaspoon tahini
250 ml (9 fl oz/1 cup) Coconut mylk (page 174)
2.5 cm (1 inch) knob of cacao butter
200 g (7 oz/1 cup) coconut sugar
2 tablespoons maca powder
1 tablespoon mesquite powder
1 tablespoon lucuma powder
2 teaspoons vanilla powder
1 tablespoon non-GM soy lecithin
pinch of Himalayan pink salt or Celtic sea salt

Chocolate topping
185 ml (6 fl oz/¾ cup) Coconut mylk (page 174)
375 ml (13 fl oz/1½ cups) cold-pressed extra virgin coconut oil
2 tablespoons non-GM soy lecithin
1 teaspoon vanilla powder
100 g (3½ oz/½ cup) coconut sugar
125 ml (4 fl oz/½ cup) coconut nectar
pinch of Himalayan pink salt or Celtic sea salt

❖ Combine all the slice base ingredients in a food processor on high speed until the mixture starts to bind to itself. Line a rectangular baking dish, measuring about 32 x 22 cm (12½ x 8½ inches) and about 5 cm (2 inches) deep, with plastic wrap. Press the mixture into the dish.
❖ Blend all the caramel ingredients in a high-speed blender until smooth. Pour the caramel over the base and set in the freezer for 2 hours.

❖ Once the caramel has set, blend up all the topping ingredients until smooth and glossy, then pour over the caramel layer. Gently tap the cake tin on a hard surface to remove air bubbles, and for a nice level finish. Refrigerate for 30 minutes.
❖ To serve, leave at room temperature for 15 minutes, then cut into portions.
❖ The slice will keep in an airtight container in the fridge for 5 days, or can be frozen for several months.

KEY LIME PIE

MAKES ONE 23 CM
(9 INCH) ROUND PIE

Key lime pie is so refreshing, and makes me feel like I'm on holidays.
If you can't get your hands on key limes, just use regular limes. It's all good.

Macadamia nut base
400 g (14 oz/2½ cups) activated
    macadamia nuts
135 g (4¾ oz/1½ cups) finely
    desiccated coconut
3 tablespoons coconut nectar
2 tablespoons lime zest
1 teaspoon vanilla powder

Lime & coconut filling
375 ml (13 fl oz/1½ cups) lime juice
2 avocados, flesh chopped
185 ml (6 fl oz/¾ cup) coconut
    nectar

185 ml (6 fl oz/¾ cup) Coconut
    mylk (page 174)
250 ml (9 fl oz/1 cup) cold-pressed
    extra virgin coconut oil
1 teaspoon spirulina powder
1 teaspoon vanilla powder
2 tablespoons non-GM soy lecithin
pinch of Himalayan pink salt or
    Celtic sea salt

To serve
twisty lime slices (see Tip) and
    lime zest, to garnish
desiccated coconut, for sprinkling

❖ Process all the nut base ingredients in a food processor until well
combined. The mixture should bind to itself when pressed together
between your fingers. Press into a 23 cm (9 inch) pie tin lined with plastic
wrap and set aside.
❖ Blend all the filling ingredients until super smooth. Pour over the pie
base, then leave to set in the fridge for 4 hours, or overnight.
❖ Remove the pie from the refrigerator. Just before serving, garnish
with twisty lime slices, lime zest and a sprinkling of desiccated coconut.
❖ The pie will keep in an airtight container in the fridge for 5 days, or
can be frozen for several months.

 To make twisty lime slices, cut a slit into each lime slice, running from
the centre to the outside. Take the two ends from either side of the slit
and twist them in opposite directions.

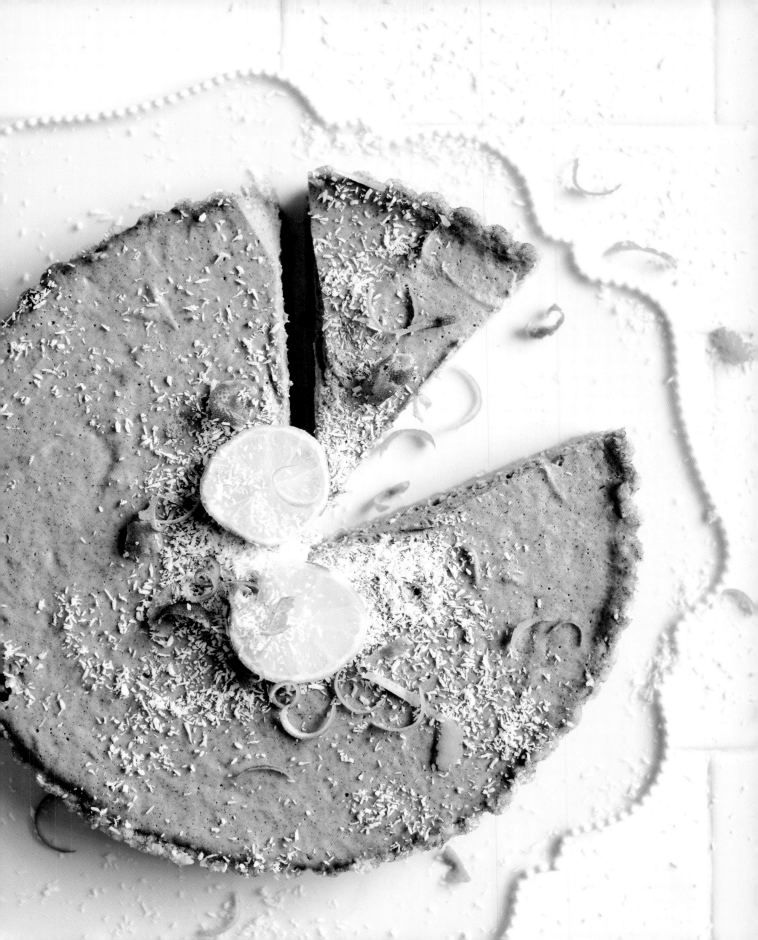

WAFFLE BOWL SUNDAES WITH BANANA SOFT SERVE

SERVES 6–8

A fun take on the traditional sundae, without all the refined sugar and dairy.
Get the kids involved by letting them prepare their own mix-ins and toppings.
You can top these sundaes with whatever you like, to create endless variations.

Waffle bowls
310 g (11 oz/2 cups) activated
cashew nuts
620 g (1 lb 6 oz/4 cups) activated
almonds
110 g (3¾ oz/1 cup) linseed
(flaxseed) meal
110 g (3¾ oz/1 cup) raw cacao
powder
2 over-ripe bananas
1 tablespoon vanilla powder

½ teaspoon Himalayan pink salt
or Celtic sea salt
40 g (1½ oz/½ cup) chopped
young coconut flesh
250 ml (9 fl oz/1 cup) coconut
nectar
150 g (5½ oz/¾ cup) coconut sugar

Banana soft serve
6–8 bananas, chopped and frozen
1 teaspoon ground cinnamon

To serve
250 g (9 oz) strawberries,
hulled and sliced
3 tablespoons cacao nibs
1 batch Salted caramel sauce
(page 142)
1 batch Chocolate fudge sauce
(page 147)
6–8 cherries

❖ Start by making the waffle bowls. Grind the cashews, then the almonds, to a flour using a high-speed blender, transferring each batch to a food processor.
❖ Add all the remaining waffle bowl ingredients to the food processor and mix until a dough forms. Press some of the dough into a small silicone bowl to mould it into a bowl shape; you can also use any small glass bowl lined with plastic wrap for this.
❖ Pop the waffle bowl out of the mould and carefully press the outside surfaces of the bowl onto a mesh dehydrator tray to give a waffle-like texture.
❖ Repeat to make more waffle bowls out of the remaining mixture.

❖ Place the waffle bowls on mesh dehydrator trays. Dehydrate at 40°C (105°F) for 8 hours. (If you don't have a dehydrator, place the waffle bowls on a baking tray and leave in the oven on its lowest setting, with the door slightly ajar, for 2 hours.)
❖ When the waffle bowls are ready, place all the banana soft serve ingredients in a food processor and blend until thick and creamy.
❖ Scoop into the waffle bowls and decorate with some sliced strawberries and cacao nibs. Add a drizzle of salted caramel sauce and chocolate fudge sauce. Finish with a cherry on top and serve.

CARAMEL CHEEZECAKE

MAKES ONE 23 CM (9 INCH) ROUND CAKE

When you need to bring a contribution to a raw vegan pot-luck gathering, whip up this simple but impressive cheezecake. I mean, don't you hate it when you have nothing on hand, and you end up being the person who only brings a plate of fruit? Make this instead, because it's delicious and easy.

Nutty caramel base
40 g (1½ oz/¼ cup) activated almonds
80 g (2¾ oz/½ cup) activated cashew nuts
45 g (1½ oz/¼ cup) activated buckwheat groats
90 g (3¼ oz/1 cup) finely desiccated coconut
180 g (6 oz/1 cup) pitted medjool dates
4 tablespoons coconut nectar
1 tablespoon tahini
½ teaspoon maca powder
½ teaspoon lucuma powder
½ teaspoon mesquite powder

Coco caramel filling
310 g (11 oz/2 cups) activated cashew nuts
30 g (1 oz/½ cup) shredded coconut
185 ml (6 fl oz/¾ cup) cold-pressed extra virgin coconut oil
125 ml (4 fl oz/½ cup) coconut nectar
375 ml (13 fl oz/1½ cups) Coconut mylk (page 174)
1 teaspoon vanilla powder
1 tablespoon non-GM soy lecithin
2 teaspoons maca powder
2 teaspoons lucuma powder
2 teaspoons mesquite powder
pinch of Himalayan pink salt or Celtic sea salt

To finish
1 batch Salted caramel sauce (page 142), in a squeeze bottle
1 batch Chocolate fudge sauce (page 147), in a squeeze bottle

❖ Process the nutty caramel base ingredients in a food processor until well combined. The mixture should bind to itself when pressed together between your fingers. Press into a 23 cm (9 inch) round spring-form cake tin.
❖ Put all the coco caramel filling ingredients in a high-speed blender jug, mixing them with a spatula for easy blending. Blend on high speed until smooth, but for no more than 20 seconds at a time, so you don't burn out the motor.
❖ Pour the filling over the base, then gently tap the cake tin on a hard surface to get rid of air bubbles.
❖ Drizzle the salted caramel and chocolate fudge sauces over the filling layer. Use a toothpick to marble the sauces into the filling, creating pretty patterns.
❖ Set in the fridge overnight, or in the freezer for at least 4 hours.
❖ If serving from the freezer, use a hot knife to ease the cheezecake out of the tin, then let the cake sit at room temperature for 15 minutes before cutting.
❖ The cake will keep in an airtight container in the fridge for 5 days, or can be frozen for several months.

MANGO FLOAT CHEEZECAKE

MAKES ONE 23 CM (9 INCH) ROUND CAKE

'Mango float' is a Filipino dessert made with condensed milk, heavy cream, mangoes, sugary biscuits and sugar — lots and lots of refined white sugar. This version is a tribute to my food heritage, and stands as a glowing example that with raw food, you really *can* have your cake and eat it too... and not have to feel bad about it! This is still one of the most popular cakes at Sadhana Kitchen, and also a winner with my family because it's just like the mango floats we had growing up, but actually serves a nutritional purpose too. And doesn't make the kiddies go crazy after eating it.

Walnut coconut base
80 g (2¾ oz/½ cup) activated almonds
80 g (2¾ oz/½ cup) activated cashew nuts
150 g (5½ oz/1½ cups) activated walnuts
90 g (3¼ oz/1 cup) finely desiccated coconut
360 g (12¾ oz/2 cups) pitted medjool dates
4 tablespoons coconut nectar

Creamy mango filling
620 g (1 lb 6 oz/4 cups) activated cashew nuts
90 g (3¼ oz/1 cup) finely desiccated coconut
500 ml (17 fl oz/2 cups) cold-pressed extra virgin coconut oil
185 ml (6 fl oz/¾ cup) coconut nectar
2 teaspoons vanilla powder
4 tablespoons non-GM soy lecithin
4 mango cheeks, skins removed

750 ml (26 fl oz/3 cups) filtered alkaline water
pinch of Himalayan pink salt or Celtic sea salt

To serve
4 large mangoes, flesh cut into wedges
edible flowers, to garnish (optional)

❖ Process all the walnut coconut base ingredients in a food processor until well combined. The mixture should bind to itself when pressed together between your fingers. Reserve about 1 cup of the mixture, then press the rest into a 23 cm (9 inch) round spring-form cake tin.

❖ Put all the filling ingredients in a blender jug, mixing them with a spatula for easy blending. Blend on high speed until smooth, but for no more than 20 seconds at a time, so you don't burn out the motor.

❖ Pour half the filling mixture over the base, then gently tap the cake tin on a hard surface to get rid of bubbles. Sprinkle with the reserved base mixture.

❖ Set in the freezer for at least 2 hours.

❖ Remove the cheezecake base from the freezer and pour the remaining filling mixture over the top. Leave to set in the fridge overnight, or in the freezer for at least 4 hours.

❖ If serving from the freezer, use a hot knife to ease the cheezecake out of the tin, then let the cake sit at room temperature for 15 minutes before plating. Just before serving, arrange the mango slices on top, and garnish with edible flowers if desired.

❖ Without the fresh mango topping and garnishes, the cake will keep in an airtight container in the fridge for 5 days, or can be frozen for several months.

NUT & SEED MYLKS

BECAUSE WE AREN'T BABY COWS

Vegans often use the word 'mylk' to refer to the creamy juice extracted from various nuts such as almonds and cashews, as a way of differentiating this vegan product from animal milk. Apart from being acid-forming in the body, dairy milk contains the protein casein, which is not easily digested by the body. Nut and seed mylks contain an array of vitamins and minerals, and are pretty damn delicious. What's more, they're really inexpensive and easy to make, and go down a treat with the littlies.

These days, most health food stores sell special fine-meshed bags for making nut mylks at home, but you can simply squeeze the nut mylk through a clean, unused stocking or piece of muslin (cheesecloth) instead.

VANILLA ALMOND MYLK

**MAKES 750 ML
(26 FL OZ/3 CUPS)**

This is my go-to recipe when I want a simple, delicious mylk where I would once have used dairy milk. The flavour is subtle and goes nicely with granola, tea or cold-brew coffee, and in superfood smoothies in place of filtered alkaline water. It's really quite inexpensive to make, and better tasting than anything you can buy ready-made.

Also try the strawberry variation below. This creamy pink drink is filled with beautifying goodness from healthy fats, antioxidants and vitamins A and C.

155 g (5½ oz/1 cup) activated almonds
750 ml (26 fl oz/3 cups) filtered alkaline water
2 tablespoons coconut nectar, or 2 pitted medjool dates
seeds from 1 vanilla bean, or 1 teaspoon vanilla powder
pinch of Himalayan pink salt or Celtic sea salt

❖ Place everything in a high-speed blender, add a bunch of good vibes and blend on high speed until smooth. Pour through a fine-meshed strainer, or squeeze through a nut milk bag before serving.
❖ You can save the pulp in a sealed container in the fridge and use it in cookies and granola.
❖ The mylk will keep in clean, airtight glass jars in the fridge for up to 5 days.

Strawberry fields almond mylk
1 batch Vanilla almond mylk (see above)
150 g (5½ oz/1 cup) strawberries, hulled

❖ Add the mylk and strawberries to a high-speed blender and blend on high speed until smooth. Filter as instructed above. Store in clean glass jars in the fridge for up to 5 days.

COCONUT MYLK

**MAKES 750 ML
(26 FL OZ/3 CUPS)**

Coconut mylk is super creamy and loaded with electrolytes, vitamins, minerals and healthy fats. This is another awesome alternative for people with nut sensitivities or allergies. It's my favourite mylk to brew with chai.

liquid and flesh from 1 young coconut
500 ml (17 fl oz/2 cups) filtered alkaline water
2 tablespoons coconut nectar, or 2 pitted medjool dates
pinch of Himalayan pink salt or Celtic sea salt

❖ Place everything in a high-speed blender, add a bunch of good vibes and blend on high speed until smooth. Pour through a fine-meshed strainer, or squeeze through a nut milk bag before serving.
❖ The mylk will keep in clean, airtight glass jars in the fridge for up to 5 days.

OMEGA MYLK

MAKES 750 ML
(26 FL OZ/3 CUPS)

A great alternative for those who can't eat nuts due to allergies, omega mylk is high in protein and healthy fats.

120 g (4¼ oz/1 cup) hemp seeds
750 ml (26 fl oz/3 cups) filtered alkaline water
2 tablespoons coconut nectar, or 2 pitted medjool dates
pinch of Himalayan pink salt or Celtic sea salt

❖ Place everything in a high-speed blender, add a bunch of good vibes and blend on high speed until smooth. Pour through a fine-meshed strainer, or squeeze through a nut milk bag before serving.
❖ The mylk will keep in clean, airtight glass jars in the fridge for up to 5 days.

MACADAMIA MYLK

MAKES 750 ML
(26 FL OZ/3 CUPS)

Macadamias are probably my favourite nut. They're a great source of thiamine and manganese, and also contain calcium and iron. This mylk is delicious as a base for a hot chocolate.

160 g (5½ oz/1 cup) activated macadamia nuts
750 ml (26 fl oz/3 cups) filtered alkaline water
2 tablespoons coconut nectar, or 2 pitted medjool dates
pinch of Himalayan pink salt or Celtic sea salt

❖ Place everything in a high-speed blender, add a bunch of good vibes and blend on high speed until smooth. Pour through a fine-meshed strainer, or squeeze through a nut milk bag before serving.
❖ The mylk will keep in clean, airtight glass jars in the fridge for up to 5 days.

1 CHOC CASHEW MYLK

2 COCONUT MYLK

3 STRAWBERRY FIELDS
ALMOND MYLK

4 MACADAMIA MYLK

5 MAZ'S MY-LO

6 SALTED CARAMEL
ESPRESSO ALMOND MYLK

Recipes pages 174–179

5

4

6

MAZ'S MY-LO

SERVES 1; MAKES 500 ML (17 FL OZ/2 CUPS)

As a small kid, I loved chocolate drinks. This version is so satisfying, yet filled with organic plant-based wholefoods and superfood powders. No extra sugar, no harmful additives, no chemicals you can't pronounce. Just good old-fashioned wholesome ingredients that make a delicious and nutritious drink. Get into it.

400 ml (14 fl oz) of your favourite nut mylk (I use Macadamia mylk, page 175)
2 cups ice cubes (see Tip)
4 heaped tablespoons raw cacao powder, plus extra for dusting
2 tablespoons coconut sugar
1 teaspoon maca powder
1 teaspoon mesquite powder
2 tablespoons shredded coconut

❖ Blend all the ingredients in a high-speed blender until smooth, then pour into a large glass or jar to serve. Dust with extra cacao powder.
❖ Enjoy straightaway because it's so damn good!

 TIP ➤ In cooler weather, you can omit the ice and blend the ingredients for longer — basically until the blender jug is warm to touch. High-speed blenders are so powerful that the friction of the blades spinning against the jug's contents creates heat. You can use this same technique to make warm raw soups.

CASHEW MYLKS

MAKES 750 ML (26 FL OZ/3 CUPS)

Here are two delicious types of Cashew mylks. The chocolatey one is sure to please even the fussiest nut-mylk naysayer. Unless, of course, they don't like chocolate, in which case you've got a far bigger problem on your hands.

The chai-spiced one has a spicy kick from the ginger. I love drinking it with raw-food cookies, or using it to soak some chia seeds to make a delicious chai chia pudding.

155 g (5½ oz/1 cup) activated cashew nuts
750 ml (26 fl oz/3 cups) filtered alkaline water
4 tablespoons coconut nectar
seeds from 1 vanilla bean (see Tip on page 179), or 1 teaspoon vanilla powder

Choc cashew mylk
2 heaped tablespoons raw cacao powder
1 tablespoon carob powder
pinch of Himalayan pink salt or Celtic sea salt

Chai-spiced cashew mylk
4 green cardamom pods
1 teaspoon ground cinnamon
2.5 cm (1 inch) knob of fresh ginger, peeled and chopped

❖ Place the cashews, water and coconut nectar in a high-speed blender, along with the vanilla seeds or powder. Add either the Choc cashew mylk or Chai-spiced cashew mylk ingredients, then blend on high speed until smooth.
❖ Pour through a fine-meshed strainer, or squeeze through a nut milk bag before serving.
❖ The mylk will keep in clean, airtight glass jars in the fridge for up to 5 days.

CHOC MYLKS

MAKES 750 ML
(26 FL OZ/3 CUPS)

The Choc sesame mylk is like a peanut butter cup, but in drink form. The Choc hazelnut version is a healthy, nutrient-dense delight when I'm feeling the urge to get my choc-hazelnut on.

4 tablespoons coconut nectar
750 ml (26 fl oz/3 cups) filtered alkaline water
1 tablespoon carob powder
seeds from 1 vanilla bean (see Tip), or 1 teaspoon
    vanilla powder

Choc sesame mylk
115 g (4 oz/¾ cup) white sesame seeds
2 heaped tablespoons raw cacao powder
pinch of Himalayan pink salt or Celtic sea salt

Choc hazelnut mylk
140 g (5 oz/1 cup) activated hazelnuts
3 heaped tablespoons raw cacao powder

❖ Place the coconut nectar, water and carob powder in a high-speed blender, along with the vanilla seeds or powder. Add either the Choc sesame mylk or Choc hazelnut mylk ingredients, then blend on high speed until smooth.
❖ Pour through a fine-meshed strainer, or squeeze through a nut milk bag before serving.
❖ The mylk will keep in clean, airtight glass jars in the fridge for up to 5 days.

 TIP If using vanilla seeds from a vanilla bean, keep the left-over vanilla pod in a jar of coconut sugar; it will add a lovely hint of natural vanilla to the sugar.

SALTED CARAMEL ESPRESSO ALMOND MYLK

MAKES 1 LITRE
(35 FL OZ/4 CUPS)

This is the best kind of cold-brew coffee I've ever had. To cold-brew coffee, grab some freshly ground coffee beans and steep them overnight in a coffee plunger or cold-brew tower.

1 batch Vanilla almond mylk (page 174)
250 ml (9 fl oz/1 cup) cold-brew coffee
4 tablespoons coconut nectar
1 teaspoon tahini
1 teaspoon maca powder
1 teaspoon mesquite powder
1 teaspoon lucuma powder
2 pinches of Himalayan pink salt or Celtic sea salt

❖ Place everything in a high-speed blender, add a bunch of good vibes and blend on high speed until smooth. Pour through a fine-meshed strainer, or squeeze through a nut milk bag before serving.
❖ The mylk will keep in clean, airtight glass jars in the fridge for up to 5 days.

WARM TONICS & COLD ELIXIRS

Comforting and healing, the warm tonics in this chapter are great examples of using food as medicine. I enjoy one of these tonics almost every day, especially during the change of seasons, or when everyone around me is unwell — and I always seem to avoid the worst of whatever bugs are circulating. The cool medicinal elixirs are ideal when you don't feel like a hot drink, but would still relish a rich dose of nutrition.

SUPERFOOD TEA BASE

MAKES 2 LITRES
(70 FL OZ/8 CUPS)

This potent yet tasty tea is what I use as the base in all my tonics. Simply brew it up in large amounts and store it in clean glass bottles in the fridge; it will keep for 5 days. Containing cat's claw, horsetail, pau d'arco and goji berries, it offers a range of powerful antiviral, antimicrobial, antioxidant and immune-boosting properties.

4 heaped tablespoons pau d'arco tea
4 heaped tablespoons cat's claw tea
4 heaped tablespoons horsetail tea
4 heaped tablespoons goji berries
2 litres (70 fl oz/8 cups) filtered alkaline water

❖ Place all the ingredients in a large saucepan and bring to the boil. Reduce the heat and simmer for 20 minutes, then remove the pan from the heat. Allow to cool to room temperature.
❖ Pour into clean glass bottles and store in the fridge. Your superfood tea base will keep for up to 5 days.

CHOC HUG-IN-A-MUG TONIC

SERVES 1; MAKES 500 ML
(17 FL OZ/2 CUPS)

Comforting and energising, this tonic is a supercharged version of a hot chocolate. Sit back, take a sip and take flight, 'cos this little concoction will get you high, without the nasty caffeine crash.

500 ml (17 fl oz/2 cups) Superfood tea base (see left)
3 tablespoons raw cacao powder
1 teaspoon maca powder
2 teaspoons lucuma powder
1 teaspoon mesquite powder
1 tablespoon cold-pressed extra virgin coconut oil
½ teaspoon chaga extract (see Tip, page 186)
½ teaspoon he shou wu extract (see Tip, page 186)

❖ Place all the ingredients in a high-speed blender and blend on high speed until smooth. Keep blending until the heat builds and warms the liquid.
❖ Pour into a mug and enjoy straightaway.

CHEEKY CHAI TONIC

SERVES 1; MAKES 500 ML
(17 FL OZ/2 CUPS)

Reishi mushroom extract is an effective anti-stress agent. Find some time to be with yourself and enjoy this cheeky chai as you unwind and chill out.

200 ml (7 fl oz) Superfood tea base (page 182)
300 ml (10½ fl oz) Chai-spiced cashew mylk (page 178)
1 tablespoon cold-pressed extra virgin coconut oil
2 teaspoons coconut sugar
1 teaspoon grated fresh ginger
½ teaspoon reishi mushroom extract

❖ Place all the ingredients in a high-speed blender and blend on high speed until smooth. Keep blending until the heat builds and warms the liquid.
❖ Pour into a mug, settle back and enjoy.

LEMON & GINGER TONIC

SERVES 1; MAKES 500 ML
(17 FL OZ/2 CUPS)

When you feel that tickle in your throat, here's a tonic that will help soothe it, while giving your immunity a bit of a boost.

450 ml (16 fl oz) Superfood tea base (page 182)
juice of 1 lemon
2.5 cm (1 inch) knob of fresh ginger, peeled and chopped
pinch of cayenne pepper
2 tablespoons coconut nectar

❖ Place all the ingredients in a high-speed blender and blend on high speed until smooth. Keep blending until the heat builds and warms the liquid.
❖ Pour into a mug and sip away.

THE MASON ELIXIR

SERVES 1; MAKES 500 ML
(17 FL OZ/2 CUPS)

This recipe is named after my good friend Mason, one of the happiest and healthiest people I know. He was one of the first people to share the power of using food as medicine with me. This elixir basically personifies him, in liquid form.

350 ml (12 fl oz) Superfood tea base (page 182)
3 heaped tablespoons raw cacao powder
1 tablespoon hemp seeds
1 tablespoon goji berries
1 teaspoon maca powder
1 teaspoon lucuma powder
1 teaspoon cold-pressed extra virgin coconut oil
30 g (1 oz/¼ cup) frozen raspberries
110 g (3¾ oz/½ cup) frozen strawberries
½ teaspoon he shou wu extract (see Tip)
½ teaspoon chaga extract (see Tip)

❖ Place all the ingredients in a high-speed blender and blend on high speed until super smooth.
❖ Pour into a tall glass and enjoy.

 TIP He shou wu is derived from the root of a plant that grows in the mountains of China. Rich in iron, antioxidants and zinc, it is widely used in Chinese herbalism to support the liver, blood, kidneys, muscles, tendons, bones and nerves. Chaga is a medicinal mushroom rich in phytochemicals and nutrients, with potent antioxidant and immune-building properties.

THE IMMORTAL ELIXIR

SERVES 1; MAKES 500 ML
(17 FL OZ/2 CUPS)

An epic antioxidant and beautifying blend, this elixir is also great for boosting your energy and is an awesome pre-workout drink.

350 ml (12 fl oz) Superfood tea base (page 182)
½ teaspoon ground cinnamon
2 tablespoons shredded coconut
2 large medjool dates, pitted
1 teaspoon maca powder
1 teaspoon lucuma powder
1 teaspoon cold-pressed extra virgin coconut oil
25 g (1 oz/¼ cup) frozen blueberries
½ frozen banana
½ teaspoon shilajit extract

❖ Place all the ingredients in a high-speed blender and blend on high speed until super smooth.
❖ Pour into a tall glass and enjoy.

ANTI-FLU TONIC

SERVES 1; MAKES 500 ML
(17 FL OZ/2 CUPS)

When I feel a little under the weather, or when everyone around me seems to be, this is the concoction I sip on, to keep the bugs at bay. The best part is that it's actually mighty tasty, so it's more like a treat than medicine!

450 ml (16 fl oz) Superfood tea base (page 182)
juice of 1 lemon
1 tablespoon cold-pressed extra virgin coconut oil
2 tablespoons finely desiccated coconut
1 cm (½ inch) knob of fresh turmeric, peeled and chopped
1 cm (½ inch) knob of fresh ginger, peeled and chopped
2 tablespoons coconut nectar

❖ Place all the ingredients in a high-speed blender and blend on high speed until smooth. Keep blending until the heat builds and warms the liquid.
❖ Pour into a mug and enjoy.

MAZ'S FIX-ALL ELIXIR

SERVES 1; MAKES 500 ML
(17 FL OZ/2 CUPS)

I love sipping on this delicious elixir whenever I wake up with a bit of a dry or itchy throat, or feel a little cough coming on, or when the weather suddenly turns super cold.

250 ml (9 fl oz/1 cup) Superfood tea base (page 182)
200 ml (7 fl oz) Vanilla almond mylk (page 174)
5 cm (2 inch) knob of fresh ginger, peeled and chopped
2.5 cm (1 inch) knob of fresh turmeric, peeled and chopped
¼ teaspoon ground cinnamon
¼ teaspoon vanilla powder
pinch of cayenne pepper
2 tablespoons coconut nectar
1 tablespoon coconut oil

❖ Place all the ingredients in a high-speed blender and blend on high speed until smooth. Keep blending until the heat builds and warms the liquid.
❖ Pour through a strainer, into a mug, and enjoy.

INDEX

Published in 2016 by Murdoch Books, an imprint of Allen & Unwin

Murdoch Books Australia
83 Alexander Street, Crows Nest
NSW 2065
Phone: +61 (0)2 8425 0100
murdochbooks.com.au
info@murdochbooks.com.au

Murdoch Books UK
Erico House, 6th Floor, 93–99
Upper Richmond Road
Putney, London SW15 2TG
Phone: +44 (0) 20 8785 5995
murdochbooks.co.uk
info@murdochbooks.co.uk

For Corporate Orders & Custom Publishing contact Noel Hammond,
National Business Development Manager, Murdoch Books Australia

Publisher Corinne Roberts
Editorial Manager Jane Price
Design Madeleine Kane
Editor Katri Hilden
Photographer Ben Dearnley
Stylist Kristine Duran-Thiessen
Production Manager Alexandra Gonzalez

Text © Maz Valcorza 2016
Design © Murdoch Books 2016
Photography © Ben Dearnley 2016

ISBN 978 1 74336 623 3 Australia
ISBN 978 1 74336 641 7 UK
A cataloguing-in-publication entry is available from the catalogue
of the National Library of Australia at nla.gov.au
A catalogue record for this book is available from the British Library

Colour reproduction by Splitting Image, Colour Studio Pty Ltd, Clayton, Victoria
Printed by 1010 Printing International, China

MEASURES GUIDE: We have used 20 ml (4 teaspoon) tablespoon measures.
If you are using a 15 ml (3 teaspoon) tablespoon add an extra teaspoon of the
ingredient for each tablespoon specified.

DISCLAIMER: Hemp seeds are not considered psycho-active, and are legal to eat
in nearly every country in the world, but please check the laws in your country
before using and omit from recipes if necessary.

The publisher thanks the following for props used in the photography:
haydenyoulley.com; hubfurniture.com.au; haveyoumetmissjones.com.au;
keepresin.com.au; susansimonini.com.au

thank you

Thank you to all change makers, truth
seekers, unicorns, explorers and rebels.
Keep shining that starlight, and know
that you are supported and loved.
We are all in this together.

Thank you to the Sadhana Kitchen
crew of legends, past, present and
future. You guys are THE BEST.
Thanks to the kitchen staff who
helped me to prep the food for this
book's photography. Thank you
Sarah for everything, and thank
you Al for making me and SK look
so handsome always.

Thank you to my *satsang*, the
community I am a part of, and the
people I love for supporting me in
the work I do, and for believing
that we can make meaningful
and positive changes in our world.

Thank you Sam.

Thank you to momma, papa and Mik.

Thank you bunny.

Lokah Samastah Sukhino Bhavantu.